Ideology

Key Concepts in Political Science

GENERAL EDITOR: Leonard Schapiro

EXECUTIVE EDITOR: Peter Calvert

Other titles in the same series include:

ALREADY PUBLISHED

Martin Albrow	**Bureaucracy**
Peter Calvert	**Revolution**
Brian Chapman	**Police State**
Ioan Davies	**Social Mobility and Political Change**
Joseph Frankel	**National Interest**

IN PREPARATION

Shlomo Avineri	**Utopianism**
Stanley Benn	**Power**
Anthony H. Birch	**Representation**
Karl Deutsch	**Legitimacy**
S. E. Finer	**Dictatorship**
C. J. Friedrich	**Tradition and Authority**
Julius Gould	**Violence**
E. Kamenka and Alice Erh-Soon Tay	**Law**
J. F. Lively	**Democracy**
Robert Orr	**Liberty**
P. H. Partridge	**Consent and Consensus**
John C. Rees	**Equality**
Bernard Schaffer	**Modernization**
Leonard Schapiro	**Totalitarianism**
Henry Tudor	**Political Myth**

Ideology

John Plamenatz

Praeger Publishers

New York · Washington · London

Praeger Publishers, Inc.
111 Fourth Avenue, New York, N.Y. 10003, U.S.A.
5 Cromwell Place, London S.W.7, England

Published in the United States of America in 1970
by Praeger Publishers, Inc.
© 1970 by Pall Mall Press Limited, London, England
All rights reserved

Library of Congress Catalog Card Number: 69–12715
Printed in Great Britain

Contents

6/The Political Uses of Ideology 123

Bibliography 145

Index 147

'Key Concepts'
an Introductory Note

Political concepts are part of our daily speech—we abuse 'bureaucracy' and praise 'democracy', welcome or recoil from 'revolution'. Emotive words such as 'equality', 'dictatorship', 'élite' or even 'power' can often, by the very passions which they raise, obscure a proper understanding of the sense in which they are, or should be, or should not be, or have been used. Confucius regarded the 'rectification of names' as the first task of government. 'If names are not correct, language will not be in accordance with the truth of things', and this in time would lead to the end of justice, to anarchy and to war. One could with some truth point out that the attempts hitherto by governments to enforce their own quaint meanings on words have not been conspicuous for their success in the advancement of justice. 'Rectification of names' there must certainly be: but most of us would prefer such rectification to take place in the free debate of the university, in the competitive arena of the pages of the book or journal.

Analysis of commonly used political terms, their reassessment or their 'rectification', is, of course, normal activity in the political science departments of our universities. The idea of this series was indeed born in the course of discussion between a few university teachers of political science, of whom Professor S. E. Finer of Manchester University was one. It occurred to us that a series of short books, discussing the 'Key Concepts' in political science would serve two purposes. In universities these books could provide the kind of brief political texts which might be of assistance to students in gaining a fuller understanding of the terms which they were constantly using. But we also hoped that outside the universities there exists a reading public which has the time, the curiosity and the inclination to pause to reflect on some of

7

those words and ideas which are so often taken for granted. Perhaps even 'that insidious and crafty animal', as Adam Smith described the politician and statesman, will occasionally derive some pleasure or even profit from that more leisurely analysis which academic study can afford, and which a busy life in the practice of politics often denies.

It has been very far from the minds of those who have been concerned in planning and bringing into being the 'Key Concepts' series to try and impose (as if that were possible!) any uniform pattern on the authors who have contributed, or will contribute, to it. I, for one, hope that each author will, in his own individual manner, seek and find the best way of helping us to a fuller understanding of the concept which he has chosen to analyse. But whatever form the individual exposition may take, there are, I believe, three aspects of illumination which we can confidently expect from each volume in this series. First, we can look for some examination of the history of the concept, and of its evolution against a changing social and political background. I believe, as many do who are concerned with the study of political science, that it is primarily in history that the explanation must be sought for many of the perplexing problems of political analysis and judgement which beset us today. Second, there is the semantic aspect. To look in depth at a 'key concept' necessarily entails a study of the name which attached itself to it; of the different ways in which, and the different purposes for which, the name was used; of the way in which in the course of history the same name was applied to several concepts, or several names were applied to one and the same concept; and, indeed, of the changes which the same concept, or what appears to be the same concept, has undergone in the course of time. This analysis will usually require a searching examination of the relevant literature in order to assess the present stage of scholarship in each particular field. And thirdly, I hope that the reader of each volume in this series will be able to decide for himself what the proper and valid use should be of a familiar term in politics, and will gain, as it were, from each volume a sharper and better-tempered tool of political analysis.

There are many today who would disagree with Bismarck's view that politics can never be an exact science. I express no opinion on this much debated question. But all of us who are students of politics—and our numbers both inside and outside the universities continue to grow—will be the better for knowing what precisely we mean when we use a common political term.

London School of Economics   Leonard Schapiro
and Political Science   General Editor

Preface

When I was asked to write this book, and to keep it short, I had to decide how broadly to treat the subject, and I decided to treat it as broadly as I conveniently could, given the space at my disposal. If I had confined myself to discussing ideology in the political sense, I would have had to neglect other, more obscure but not less important, senses of the word. A political ideology need not be a class ideology, and yet many people hold that political ideologies are deeply influenced by 'class' ideologies, and that there is no understanding them properly unless we see how this is so. But to speak of 'class' ideologies is to speak of ideas and doctrines that are, or are held to be, 'socially conditioned'—and so we pass inexorably from one sense of the word to another. That is why I have thought it best to consider all the important senses, even though the attempt to distinguish between them would oblige me to raise difficult philosophical questions. Fortunately, I have had only to raise the questions and explain their relevance without attempting to answer them.

Although this book is about ideology and not about Marxism, it has a great deal to say about how Marx conceived of ideology; for it was he, more than anyone, who introduced the word into social and political theory, and he used it in all its important senses without troubling to make it clear how they differ. Later Marxists have either used the word much as he did, or have explained their uses of it by contrasting them with his; and where they have not themselves made the contrast, to make it is often the quickest way of explaining how they conceive of ideology, or of 'myths', 'derivations', 'belief-systems', etc., to use other words preferred by them.

In the first chapter I make a quick survey of the important uses of the word, trying to explain how they differ and how they are connected, and I point to some of the obscurities that so often make argument about ideologies, their functions and effects, empty or confusing. In the second chapter I try to show how the broadest conception of ideology, used to refer to all or most ideas, was born of German philosophy, of a theory of knowledge first put forward by Kant and later drastically revised by Hegel. In the third chapter I discuss in a general way the assertion, still much in favour among sociologists, that many (if not all) ideas are 'socially determined' or 'socially conditioned', and in the fourth, the assumption that ideology consists of beliefs, or rather sets of beliefs, whose function is to influence and justify certain kinds of behaviour. In the fifth chapter I consider the Marxist conception of 'class ideology', which is both richer and more confused than it is sometimes taken to be: for the term 'class ideology' covered, for Marx, not just the explicit doctrines of organized groups, but beliefs and attitudes widely shared by people unaware that they shared them and incapable of defining them. In this same chapter I discuss the notion that ideology is 'false consciousness' (that is to say, consists of illusions that those who have them cannot do without if they are to behave in ways typical of the class, profession, trade or community they belong to) and also the assertion (by no means confined to Marxists) that religion is a form of false consciousness. Not until the sixth and last chapter do I discuss the political uses of ideology, whether by governments or by groups aspiring to govern or to influence the making of policy.

The first chapter is introductory; but the five that follow become progressively less philosophical and more sociological and political. This does not mean that the later chapters deal with questions that are in themselves easier, though they are more familiar to students of society and government. I have tried to be as simple and clear as the nature of the subject allowed, and I hope that the order in which I have dealt with successive topics has helped me to achieve this purpose. If the book had been longer, it would have been fuller of examples; it is unavoidably abstract because it treats of a large subject in a short space.

I have to thank Mrs Jean Floud and Mr Alasdair Clayre, who read the first draft, for valuable suggestions; and my wife for reading through the typescript with me and helping me to express myself more clearly.

J.P.

1/The Uses of the Word

The word 'ideology', like the word 'sociology', was invented in France. It meant the science or study of ideas, and was first used to refer to a type of philosophy fashionable at the turn of the eighteenth and nineteenth centuries, a philosophy whose exponents prided themselves on not being metaphysicians. They explained all ideas as deriving ultimately from sensations. The most famous French thinker of this school was Condillac, a disciple of the British empiricists, but the epithet *idéologue* or *ideologist* was applied, not so much to him, as to men who came after him. This early meaning of the word would perhaps be even more forgotten than it is, if Napoleon had not picked on it and used it to express the impatience and even contempt of the man of action for men so much more interested than he is in abstract ideas. Thus, the word 'ideology' was French for a few decades before it became international and in the process changed its meaning. And though the meaning is altered, the word is still, quite often, used disrespectfully.

In its later, and much more important sense, it is used to refer to a set of closely related beliefs or ideas, or even attitudes, characteristic of a group or community. This is, as it were, the least that it means, though it often means more besides. A set of this kind can be restricted to a very few persons or shared by many. It can be shared by a whole people or even by several: by the peoples of Western Europe or of Asia or the Islamic world. Or it can be shared by all people everywhere during one period in history but not another. Or it can be confined to a diminutive sect found in only one small corner of the world. Indeed, a set of ideas can be peculiar to one person, and yet the word 'ideology' be applied to it quite properly—though, in that

15

case, the person whose ideas are so styled is held to be important. Certain ideas or beliefs or attitudes may be peculiar to him, but they affect his actions and what he does has grave consequences for others. Or, though his 'ideology', taken as a whole, is peculiar to him, some parts of it are shared by others over whom his influence is great. Thus, at times, we find it convenient to speak of the ideology of Lenin as distinct from that of the Bolsheviks, or the ideology of Calvin as distinct from that of the Calvinists. Nevertheless, ordinarily, when we speak of an ideology we have in mind a set of ideas or beliefs or attitudes characteristic of a group. The set may also be found outside the group, but presumably much less so than inside it.

I have spoken of ideas, beliefs and attitudes. These are not equivalent terms. Sometimes, we say 'idea' when we might just as well say 'belief'. John's ideas about James are his beliefs about him. But by 'idea' we sometimes mean 'concept'; we mean not a belief but something used to express beliefs. We can distinguish the concept of man from any belief about man that the concept is used to express. Nevertheless, for our purpose, which is to discuss ideology, we need not emphasize this distinction. Though a concept is not a belief, it is always used to express either a belief or something else (for example, an intention or wish or attitude) whose significance depends on the beliefs of whoever expresses it. If I say, 'Shut the door', I may not use the concept 'door' to express a belief, but I use it to express a wish or to give an order which would be pointless unless I believed that there was a door there to be shut. The concepts men use correspond to their beliefs and in the course of my discussion of ideology I shall seldom need to distinguish concepts from beliefs. I shall ordinarily use the word 'ideas' to refer to concepts and beliefs indiscriminately. In so doing, I shall follow the example of all writers who speak of ideology.

An attitude, as the dictionary defines it, is a posture or a way of behaving that indicates a belief or a feeling or a disposition to act. In this broad sense of the word, animals other than man, though they do not, strictly speaking, have beliefs, do have attitudes; they have feelings and dispositions to act and we can tell what these are from their demeanour. But the attitudes we have in mind are human; they are the attitudes of creatures that use concepts and express beliefs. The feelings and dispositions they indicate are peculiar to such creatures; they arise from beliefs, or rather they arise in situations of which beliefs form an essential part. What is more, the behaviour that indicates them is predominantly verbal. Jones, when he is angry with Smith, may take up a threatening attitude without a word spoken. Indeed, he may be an idiot incapable of speech or of thought at the human level and so take up a threatening attitude much as a dog does. But when slaves or serfs take up a threatening attitude to their social superiors, they nearly always use words in doing so; and to use words is to use ideas.

Spread and comprehensiveness

Just as we can ask about the sort or the size of the group or community who are said to share an ideology, so we can ask just how many of their ideas and attitudes are included in the ideology. That is to say, we can enquire into the spread of an ideology, what sort of people or what proportion of a people or of mankind share it, or we can enquire into its comprehensiveness, into the proportion of their total ideas and attitudes that it covers. An ideology may be widely spread and be either very comprehensive or not so. There seems to be no constant correlation between the spread and the comprehensiveness of ideologies. We cannot say, the greater the spread of an ideology, the less it is comprehensive; nor can we say the opposite.

Sometimes an ideology of the most comprehensive kind is called a 'world-view', or even a *Weltanschauung*, by English and American writers who believe that there is no exact English equivalent of this German word. This notion of a 'world-view' or *Weltanschauung* or (to give it yet another name) 'total ideology', is not altogether clear. Are we to understand by it a theory, a more or less coherent system of explicit beliefs, about the world? Or are we to understand the presuppositions implicit in ordinary ways of thinking and speaking about the things and persons, the events and actions, that constitute the world? A world-view or total ideology, in the first sense, is something sophisticated that only a few members of a community or other social group may have. In the second sense, it may be shared by them all. So we must distinguish at least two levels of total ideology: sophisticated and unsophisticated.

We cannot take it for granted that the two levels correspond with one another, that a sophisticated total ideology merely makes explicit the presuppositions of an unsophisticated one. For, in a community or other group in which there are several sophisticated ideologies, there may be only one that is unsophisticated. Indeed, if all the members of the community or group are to understand one another's ordinary discourse, they must share an unsophisticated ideology.

An ideology may be partial; it may consist of ideas and attitudes that relate only to a part of reality. Indeed, ideologies are nearly always partial. Or, perhaps I should say, the word 'ideology' is nearly always used to refer to a particular sphere of thought and not to thought generally. For example, the Marxists, when they speak of 'class ideology', nearly always have in mind only some spheres of thought. Sometimes, no doubt, they claim to be doing more. But the claim, taken literally, is absurd; a class ideology cannot include all the ideas used by members of the class. Even in the most capitalist of societies, bourgeois and proletarians speak the same language—if not all the time, then much of it. The claim that the bourgeois have an all-embracing ideology characteristic of their class is plausible only if it is taken to mean that they have a total ideology of the sophisticated kind, an all-embracing philosophy.

We can distinguish also two levels of partial ideology. For example, we can distinguish the ideas used in carrying on the business of the state from the ideas used in constructing theories of the state, or the ideas used by producers and traders engaged in production and trade from the ideas of the economist.

It is sometimes extraordinarily difficult to assess either the spread or the comprehensiveness of an ideology. For example, when we hear a Marxist (or, indeed, anyone else) speaking of 'bourgeois ideology', we are often left wondering just what sections of the people, in his opinion, share the ideology, and just what spheres of thought (and at what levels) are included in it. If we invite the speaker to settle our doubts, as often as not we cause him to share them or we irritate him.

The bourgeois, presumably, does not use ideas or hold beliefs or take up attitudes characteristic of his class no matter how he thinks and acts in peculiarly human ways. Not everything that is human about him, as distinct from merely animal, is bourgeois. When he takes up gardening in his leisure hours, and acts thoughtfully in ways appropriate to a gardener, he is presumably free of bourgeois ideology, just as the proletarian engaged in the same activity is free of proletarian ideology. But if we say that the bourgeois thinks as a bourgeois only when he is engaged in social activities peculiar to his class, we then have to decide what those activities are. Which is no small task.

The bourgeois, let us say, differs from the proletarian primarily because he takes a different part in the process of production. This difference between them is perhaps the most easily defined. But the bourgeois and the proletarian have ordinarily more to do with one another at work than in their domestic or leisure hours. There is presumably a good deal that is common to their ideas and attitudes when they are engaged in production or trade, for they contrive to work intelligently together. But the bourgeois, like the proletarian, engages in more than these activities. He is also a father, a husband, a citizen and much else besides. His ideas when he acts in these other capacities may be the ones that differ most from those of the proletarian. If we try to distinguish his social activities from those of the proletarian, we may find it easier to make this distinction between their productive than between their other activities. But if we try to distinguish between their ideas, we may find it easier to do so when these relate to other than productive activities. How are we to set about the business of determining what is to count as bourgeois ideology? Must we first decide what social activities are characteristically bourgeois, and then look out for ideas much more common among persons engaged in these activities than among others? If we try to do this, we may often find it impossible to define an activity except by reference to the ideas of the persons engaged in it. Though the bourgeois' part in the process of production or the source of his income may be clearly enough distinguished from the proletarian's, with no reference made to ideas and attitudes, can his role as a father or a husband or a citizen be so too? Or can we say that most people whose source of income or role in production is typically bourgeois, when they behave as fathers, husbands or citizens, do so in ways characteristic of the economic group they belong to?

The word 'ideology', used to refer to the ideas and attitudes characteristic of a group or community, is—as we have seen— of fairly recent origin. It was used in this sense by Marx and Engels, and has come into more general use as the influence of their ideas has spread. They used it carelessly, so that often (as, for example, when they spoke of what we have just been discussing, bourgeois ideology) we cannot tell just what groups or what ideas they had in mind. They established a tradition of careless use.

Marx and Engels used the word to help them express some rather obscure, though also important, ideas they had about the connection of beliefs and attitudes, either generally or in some particular sphere, with other human activities. These ideas were not all original with them, for they took some of the best of them from Hegel, who contrived to express them without using the word 'ideology'; and Hegel had his precursors. Marx and Engels and their disciples have not been the only users of the word, nor has it been used only in the senses they gave to it.

Yet it is their word more than it is anyone else's. They were the first to give wide currency to it and even today most writers who use it or who discuss its uses, even when they are not Marxists, are very much aware of the uses of it made by Marx and his followers. Even when they are not directly concerned with the theories of Marx and Engels, they are as often as not trying to answer or reformulate questions that Marx and Engels put, or to put and answer other questions suggested by a critical analysis of Marxist views about ideology.

I said earlier that the word 'ideology' is not used to refer only to explicit beliefs and theories. Those who speak of bourgeois ideology do not always mean by it the theories and doctrines of writers whom they call bourgeois on the ground that their theories have been widely accepted among the bourgeois. They often mean by it beliefs and attitudes implicit in bourgeois ways of speaking and behaving, and sometimes they speak of bourgeois theories and doctrines as if they did little more than make explicit these beliefs and attitudes. They speak of bourgeois theorists or ideologists (as they sometimes call them) as if they were much more exponents than creators of bourgeois ideology. But they do not speak in this way consistently, for some of their explanations and arguments imply that ideologists are as much creators as exponents of ideology.

Though the term ideology is by no means confined to explicit beliefs it is in practice seldom used to refer to the beliefs of primitive peoples. I do not know why this should be so. For some reason or other, it is a word much less in favour among social anthropologists (who study primitive and mostly illiterate peoples) than among sociologists (who study more developed and literate peoples)—though there are also sociologists who prefer to speak of 'belief-systems' where they might as well speak of ideologies. Yet the distinction between explicit and implicit beliefs applies also to societies that are primitive. In these societies, of course, there are no writers of books; there are no makers of theories, no ideologists, recognized as such. But there are express beliefs as distinct from beliefs that are implicit in ways of speaking and behaving. And the express beliefs about some class of things or actions or events may form a coherent system of beliefs.

When historians and philosophers come to notice that beliefs differ greatly from one part of the world to another, from one age to another, they soon ask how this comes about. How is it that different peoples and different ages not only give different answers to the same questions but put different questions? Now this is a sophisticated question, and is put only in communities where theories abound, where philosophers and historians are critical of one another and of their predecessors, where they notice, not only how they differ among themselves, but the much greater differences between them and those who came before them or who write history and philosophy in societies different from their own. They are very much aware of one another but are aware also that they do not work in a cultural world inhabited only by themselves. They see themselves as men of ideas in a way that most men are not and yet also as belonging to cultures to which other men belong as much as they do.

So, for example, when they contrast ancient Greek ideas about man, society and government with their own, they have in mind not just the explicit beliefs of Greek writers whose works have come down to them but attitudes and sentiments more widespread than these beliefs and yet connected with them. But their evidence for what they say about these attitudes and sentiments consists for the most part of what they find in the writings and fragments that have come down to us. Thus, though ideology, as they conceive of it, is something popular and therefore not confined to deliberately constructed theories, or even express beliefs, but includes assumptions and sentiments which those who act upon them are often incapable of putting into words, they get their ideas about a particular ideology largely from the works of writers whom they take to be exponents of it. Though ideology does not consist necessarily of theories and explicit beliefs, writers who readily admit this still speak of it as if it were predominantly theoretical and explicit. The study of popular ways of thinking and feeling is of recent origin; and though the beliefs of primitive peoples described by social anthropologists are uninfluenced by theory, popular ideas and sentiments in advanced and literate societies are deeply, even though indirectly, influenced by it. As for the popular beliefs of past ages, we have access to them only if they are recorded accurately, and we cannot be sure how far they are so.

'False consciousness'

Marx often called ideology 'false consciousness'. He also spoke of it as 'determined' by social conditions or 'social existence'. And yet, so it would appear, he did not think it was false consciousness because so determined. For he held, at least sometimes, that consciousness in general, and not just false consciousness, is determined by social existence. What he meant by 'consciousness' no doubt varied with the context, but he seems at times to have used it in the broadest possible sense to cover all ideas and beliefs. Consciousness, thus broadly conceived, cannot be all false consciousness. So ideology, if it is false consciousness, is only a part of consciousness.

Later I shall return to this obscure doctrine that consciousness is determined by social existence. I shall consider it in a general way and not only Marx's version of it. But now I want to look at this idea of false consciousness. False consciousness is not just any kind of false belief. A scientist, competently and conscientiously using methods appropriate to his kind of enquiry, may reach a false conclusion which he believes to be true. His belief, though it concerns not just one event but any event of a given kind, is not a case of false consciousness. Nor are the mistaken beliefs of ordinary life cases of false consciousness. The man who believes it is three o'clock when actually it is two is not falsely conscious. By false consciousness, Marx appears to have meant a set of mistaken beliefs about matters important to them shared by a whole group of persons or even a whole community. False consciousness is pervasive and has extensive social consequences. It consists of a number of closely related illusions common to all or nearly all persons whose situations or roles in society are the same. Bourgeois ideas about the state are, so Marx believed, an example of false consciousness. Presumably, he meant not all their political ideas but only some. The belief in the sovereignty of the Queen in Parliament, which in Marx's time was more widely understood and accepted by the middle than by the working classes, was not false. Any competent lawyer could have given an account of this sovereignty as acceptable to Marx as to anyone else capable of understanding it. The beliefs that Marx thought were illusory were beliefs about the essential functions of the state. He appears to have believed that these false beliefs were necessary to enable the state to carry out its real functions. If the state is to be what it really is, if it is to favour the interests which in fact it does favour, there must be false beliefs more or less widely accepted about what it is, about the interests it favours. For example, it must be widely held that it favours interests common to all who are subject to its authority, whereas in fact, according to Marx, it favours the interests of one class to the detriment of others.

This conception of ideology as false consciousness has attracted other than Marxist thinkers. Where Marxists speak of 'ideologies', Pareto speaks of 'derivations'. A 'derivation' is a theory, or at least a closely related set of beliefs, that people accept, regardless of its truth, because it serves to justify, and to some extent even to direct, their activities. Pareto did not think of these activities as a pursuit of group interests; indeed, he thought of them as being for the most part not rational—or not logical, as he preferred to put it. His 'derivations' do not therefore serve to justify the pursuit of class or other group interests as ideologies do, according to the Marxists and others who think as they do. Nor did Pareto say that 'derivations' are made up largely of false beliefs; he was concerned rather to argue that they are accepted for other reasons than because they have been critically examined and found to be true.

Sorel was impressed by the power of social and political 'myths'. It is pointless, so he thought, to enquire how far they are true. They are accepted because they express the sentiments of those who accept them; they are outlets for feelings and excuses for action. In calling them so, he did not mean to disparage them. He was not, as Pareto was or affected to be, 'au-dessus de la mêlée'; he did not claim to be a dispassionate observer of myths and their social consequences. His sympathies, like those of Marx, were with the proletariat, whom he thought of as a revolutionary class. He rejoiced in its being so. Yet he did not look upon its revolution as a pursuit of class interests; he thought of it rather as a gesture, as an act of self-assertion, as something done for its own sake. The proletarians make the revolution because they are impelled to do so, because their place in society is such that they feel the need to assert themselves as a class by making it. The myth, accepted regardless of its truth, justifies and defines the gesture which they make. In the eyes of Sorel, both the revolution and the myth take on the character almost of works of art, though the artist is not an individual but a class.

Marx did not trouble to distinguish between the elements that go to make up an ideology, and therefore did not enquire whether all of them can properly be subsumed under 'false consciousness'. For example, he spoke of morality as 'ideological'. But moral rules are not themselves false beliefs, even though it should turn out that many of the beliefs that people have about them are false, or that part of the process of educating people to keep moral rules consists in getting them to accept beliefs that are false or unverifiable.

False consciousness or myth can have a variety of functions. Sometimes, though by no means always, Marx speaks of ideology, when he calls it false consciousness, as if its prime function were to promote class interests. The ideologies of dominant or

exploiting classes promote their interests by justifying the established order which is the condition of their predominance or
exploitation; the ideologies of oppressed and exploited classes
challenge that order. The myths that Sorel speaks of, though
they are class ideologies, do not (at least not in the Marxist
sense) promote class interests. Pareto's 'derivations' are conceived more generally as group ideologies; they serve to bring
and hold together people who have similar ambitions, impulses
and attitudes rather than to promote interests common to them.
That is to say, they serve to create and maintain groups rather
than to sustain them in the pursuit of their group interests. The
'governing class', as Pareto conceives of it, does not consist of
people who are united by common interests or common beliefs
—though they may well have some interests and beliefs in common just as they may have some in common with the subject
classes. It consists rather of élites who, because they are formid-
able, must take much greater account of one another than they
need take of groups outside the governing class.

Clearly, the 'bearers' of an ideology or a myth need not be a
social class; they may be a group different in kind from what
Marxists or anyone else would call a class. They may be a group
much smaller than a class or they may be an entire community.
Marx himself admitted this, at least by implication. He called
religion 'ideology' and also 'false consciousness', and did not
deny that there are religions in primitive and classless societies.
Today all students of society recognize the importance of myths
(or part-myths) in preserving the character of a community or
of some aspect or other of its life in which everyone shares.
These myths are not class or sectional ideologies but are com-
munal. And yet they are examples of what Marx understood by
false consciousness.

Marx and Engels did not use the word 'ideology' to refer to
their own theory, even though, in their opinion, it was a theory
in line with the class interests of the proletariat, and therefore a
theory that the proletariat would gradually come to accept as

it learned to recognize its class interests. They did not call their theory an ideology presumably because they did not think of it as a form of false consciousness. The proletariat, according to them, is in one respect a uniquely privileged class: the beliefs about society and the course of social change that favour its interests are true beliefs. Indeed, it is a condition of proletarians recognizing the real interests of their own class that they should hold these beliefs. It is their destiny to be the only class that understands the course of social change and rises above false consciousness.

This theme is less prominent in the writings of Marx than in those of the Hungarian, Georg Lukacs, whom many regard as the most profound and imaginative Marxist thinker of the twentieth century. In his book, *History and Class Consciousness* (1900), Lukacs explains more systematically than Marx did in what respects the role of the proletariat, as a revolutionary class, is unique. Lukacs does not use the term 'proletarian ideology' but speaks always of the class consciousness of the proletariat. Other Marxist writers of our century have not followed his example; they have been ready to speak of proletarian or of Communist ideology. But this does not mean that they have admitted that it too, like bourgeois ideology, is false consciousness or myth. On this issue, all Marxists stand with Marx and with Lukacs, not with Sorel or Pareto. Truth, they think, is in a special sense the ally of the proletariat.

A family of concepts

Though 'ideology' has several meanings, sometimes difficult to distinguish from one another, the meanings are closely related. The word is always used to refer to a system of ideas or beliefs that the user thinks of as in some way limited. Even a 'total ideology' is limited; it consists of the ideas and beliefs of a particular people or group of peoples, or a particular epoch. It is confined to them; it is the world as they see it, as it appears to them. Even if it is held to include all their ideas and beliefs, and therefore to be quite literally a *total* ideology, it is still only one such ideology among others. As a matter of fact, as we shall see later, even writers who speak of a 'total ideology'—or who speak in a general way of 'thought' or 'consciousness' as if it were 'ideological' or in some way peculiar to a particular people or age, or even species—scarcely ever do so consistently. They take up on occasion an extreme position only to retreat from it later.

Ideology, in the broadest sense, since it includes all the ideas and beliefs of a people, cannot be distinguished from thought that is not ideological. But it can be distinguished from a people's other social activities; or, perhaps I should say, from other aspects of their social activities, since all man's social activities involve thinking. This distinction, as I hope to show later, is very difficult—perhaps impossible—to make, except in a quite trivial sense. Even those who try to make it sometimes concede that it really cannot be made, and yet still insist on making it. Or, sometimes, they speak as if the distinction were so obvious that merely to mention it is to be understood, and at other times as if it could not be made.

Marx, as every student of Marxism knows, distinguished social existence from consciousness, and said of it that it determines consciousness and not the other way about. He also distinguished, among man's social activities, a material substructure from an ideological superstructure, saying once again that the first determines the second. It could be argued that Marx had in mind not one distinction but two; that, in his idiom, social existence is not equivalent to the material substructure, nor consciousness to the ideological superstructure. It could also be argued, with perhaps no less support from the texts, that he had in mind only one distinction: that sometimes at least he spoke as if consciousness and ideology were the same thing. Fortunately, as our subject is ideology and not Marxism, we need not consider the merits of these arguments. There may or there may not be, somewhere in the writings of Marx, implicit the concept of 'total ideology' or the doctrine that all ideas and beliefs are significant or true only from a certain 'point of view'. It is enough to notice that some of the theorists who have come closest to putting forward this doctrine—though no one has done so unequivocally—have thought of themselves as following up implications of what Marx said.

These theorists have all hesitated to go the whole way in asserting this doctrine. At some point or other in their arguments, they have excluded the most abstract of ideas (those that the logician and the mathematician operate with) from the number that are 'culture-relative', as they sometimes put it. All other ideas and beliefs depend on 'the point of view' of the thinker, and this 'point of view' changes, being determined only in part by human physiology and for the rest by social conditions. But social conditions change continually. As Marx put it, though without seeing clearly the full implications of his own words: 'Social existence determines consciousness.' All thinking, they say, is from a 'point of view', which (as Marx rightly saw) is as much social as it is physical. But, we may ask, if they go so far as to say this, whence their reluctance to throw in, with the others, for full measure, the ideas of logic and mathematics? For these formal sciences also have their histories. Why should not their conclusions also be 'culture-relative'? I shall take up this question again in a later chapter.

Ideology in narrower senses can, of course, be distinguished from thought that is not ideological. For example, it is often distinguished from what is called 'scientific' thought and also from the thinking involved in many but not all forms of everyday practical activity: in farming, in carrying on a craft or trade, or at work and leisure within the family. The distinction here is not between theory and practice. The sciences, which are contrasted with ideology, are forms of theory. Rituals and ceremonies are practice rather than theory, and yet the ideas they express or that lend significance to them are ideological. There is a great deal of ceremony in everyday life.

The social studies, as distinct from the natural sciences, are often called ideology, or are given some other equivalent name, even when it is recognized that the persons engaged in them are seriously concerned to be objective. People call them so who hold that explanations of social behaviour are inevitably affected by the social situation or point of view of the explainer in a way that explanations of natural events are not. Moreover, the social studies affect what they study as the natural sciences do not; for what they study is human behaviour, and human behaviour is deeply affected by human beliefs about it.

When the word is used in a yet narrower sense, it is admitted that even the social studies are not, or need not be, ideological. It is conceded that they are much more apt than the natural sciences to be tainted by ideology, and that with them it is much more difficult than with explanations of natural events to decide where they cease to be properly scientific and become ideological. Nevertheless, they can in principle (so it is claimed for them) be scientific.

Some sociologists—for example, Karl Mannheim—have held that all explanations of natural events and human behaviour, as distinct from such purely formal studies as logic and mathematics, are 'culture-relative', and yet have argued that we can still distinguish among such explanations those that are scientific from those that are not. Where there are definite, consistent, usable and generally accepted criteria for testing the truth or falsity of beliefs, then it is possible to distinguish beliefs that pass the test from those that do not. It may be that the natural sciences come closer to having such criteria than the social studies do; but there is no reason, in principle, why the social studies should not also come to have them. The natural sciences have come by their criteria gradually. They have not been unchanging criteria and will no doubt change again. For science to be possible, there is no need for criteria of truth that never change; there is a need only for definite, consistent and usable criteria that are accepted at a particular period or within a particular culture by all who can understand and use them.

This, of course, does not entail that all beliefs that are not scientific are ideological. As we saw earlier, for beliefs to be ideological, in this narrower sense, they must be shared by a group of people, they must concern matters important to the group, and must be in some way functional in relation to it: they must serve to hold it together or to justify activities and attitudes characteristic of its members. Nor does it entail that no true beliefs are ideological, for true beliefs can also be functional in these ways. What makes beliefs ideological, in the sense we are now discussing, is their constituting a system of beliefs which is functional in these ways, and is therefore accepted regardless of whether or not its constituent beliefs satisfy the criteria of truth. Ideologies, in this sense, often contain many beliefs that are false or unverifiable, but they nearly always contain some true beliefs as well. An ideology is not 'ideological' in respect only of the false or unverifiable beliefs contained in it, for it is 'ideological' as a whole set of beliefs that serves to hold a group together or to justify its activities and attitudes or to promote its interests. The set of beliefs need not, and usually is not, a theory. Illiterate groups incapable of constructing theories can have ideologies. The sociologist who studies these ideologies can explain, perhaps, how their constituent beliefs fit together into more or less coherent systems, but the illiterates whose ideologies they are cannot do it.

In the remaining chapters of this book, I shall try further to elucidate these different senses of ideology and to discuss briefly some of the important issues raised by a critical examination of them. The writers who have made the largest and most varied use of the word 'ideology' (or of others equivalent to it) have not faced these issues and have perhaps been unaware of them. They have used the word carelessly, even when they have used it to say something new and important.

2/German Philosophy and the Concept of Ideology

Ideology in the broadest sense is often called by another name. What Marx contrasts, boldly but not clearly, with social existence, he calls 'consciousness' and not 'ideology'. And though he also contrasts an ideological superstructure with a material substructure, he leaves it uncertain how far, in his opinion, this superstructure is coextensive with consciousness. What makes consciousness, as he speaks of it, seem to coincide with what others have called 'total ideology' is his saying of it that it is determined by social existence. Others have said the same thing of 'thought' or 'knowledge' taken generally. This way of speaking about 'consciousness' or 'thought' or 'knowledge' derives from German philosophy or, rather, from a marriage of philosophy with history, consummated in Germany. That is to say, the concept of ideology in the broadest sense was born of that marriage, and so too were the narrower concepts. This whole family of concepts derives from the attempts by German philosophers to explain what knowledge is and how it arises.

Kant and Hegel

The eighteenth century in Britain and France was the age of empirical philosophy, and David Hume, perhaps the greatest philosopher of that school, had come close to speaking of the mind as if it were a mere flow of sense impressions and their faint copies in memory, associated in diverse ways. To know or to believe is to have or to expect such impressions and faint copies. Knowledge and belief, looked at in these ways, are not activities; rather, they are events. The mind, thus conceived, is no more active than a river whose waters move to the sea. This account of what is involved in knowing and believing seems to ignore altogether a distinction, implicit in ordinary ways of speaking about knowledge and belief, between the subject, the knower or believer, and the object, what he knows or believes. What are ordinarily spoken of as if they were acts of an enduring self, whose actions are many and varied, acts of comparing, asserting, questioning, deciding and so on, are reduced to ways in which impressions and their faint copies are connected. There is nothing 'in the mind' except what is given in sensation or traces of it, and ideas such as 'cause' and 'substance', which clearly are not sense impressions nor traces of them, are reduced to mere habits and expectations formed by experience.

Kant rejected this account of knowledge and belief, though he admired Hume's valiant attempt to take a certain kind of empiricism to its logical conclusion. Knowledge, as Kant saw it, is essentially active; it involves the making of assertions or judgements by a self-conscious being. It involves also the use of logically interdependent ideas that are not given in sensation and cannot be reduced to habits and expectations. Kant was not concerned to explain the genesis of these basic ideas; he was concerned rather to argue that assertion or judgement—that is to say, knowledge and belief as distinct from mere sensation and habitual unthinking response to it—is impossible without them. To know and to believe is necessarily to use these ideas, to apply them to what is given in sensation. If this is so, then it follows that these basic ideas are not deliberately produced, for there can be no deliberate production of ideas except by persons who are capable of making judgements and decisions, and the making of them involves the use of these ideas. These basic ideas Kant called 'categories'; and he said of them that they are *a priori* because it is only by using them that we acquire a coherent experience, an awareness of an ordered world and of ourselves as enduring persons inside it. It is as persons having this awareness that we have knowledge and belief as distinct from a mere flow of sensations. Their being *a priori* does not entail that we recognize them for what they are before we use them to create for ourselves the image of a world. For to have ideas is to use them to make assertions, even though sometimes only to oneself, and also to take decisions which—if they really are decisions and not just unthinking responses to stimuli—are based on assertions or judgements, on the sizing up of situations.

Kant, as other philosophers had done before him, held that what is given in sensation is an effect of the impact of what is external to us on our sense organs, and that we have no warrant for believing that what is 'outside' the mind looks like the impressions received by the mind. If our organs of sense were different, the products 'inside' our minds of the impact of external objects on them would also be different. So Kant distinguished things as they appear to us, which are products of our ideas applied to our sense impressions, from things as they are in themselves, the *phenomenal* from the *noumenal* world, the world as we know it from the world as it is, beyond the reach of our knowledge. He also, for reasons we need not consider, distinguished the phenomenal from the noumenal self. He did not argue, as some philosophers have tried to do, that self-knowledge is uniquely privileged, that it is knowledge of the self as it really is.

The world as we know it is the world as it necessarily appears to us. We do not choose that it shall appear as it does. And yet it is also, in a sense, a world of our making. Our sense impressions are 'in our minds', even though they are effects upon us of what is external to us; and it is we who produce the phenomenal world by applying our ideas to them. We do not create this world of appearances as God, according to some theologians, creates the real world; we do not first conceive of it and then bring it into existence. Still, it is a product of our activities, of how we apply our ideas to our sensations.

Creatures with organs of sense different from ours would receive different sense impressions, and it is at least conceivable that, if they were rational creatures, if they could acquire knowledge of an ordered world, they might use in acquiring it basic ideas or categories in some respects different from the ones that Kant discussed. Kant did not amuse himself by considering this possibility, and I do not know whether he thought of his categories as involved necessarily in any coherent experience of a world or only in human experience. But he did look upon our phenomenal world as being a stable unchanging world: the world as it necessarily appears to such creatures as we are. It is the world as it appears to men in all places and at all times. But, notoriously, men's theories and beliefs about one aspect or other of the world differ greatly, and are inconsistent with one another. It would seem therefore to follow that all these theories and beliefs presuppose one and the same basic image of the world. If they are inconsistent only with one another, they may all make sense, though some must be false; but if any are inconsistent with this basic image, they do not make sense. Since Kant assumed that his categories are involved in all human thinking about the world, he did not explain how we come to have them. He did not enquire whether, and to what extent, they are affected by our needs and social conditions. There is nothing in his philosophy that corresponds to Marx's distinction between social existence and consciousness.

Hegel thought it absurd to distinguish a phenomenal world that we can know, a world of appearances, from a noumenal world of things as they really are beyond the reach of our knowledge. It makes sense to distinguish the apparent from the real only if the real is knowable, for we cannot recognize the merely apparent for what it is unless we can account for its being as it is. But to account for its being as it is, is to explain how, under such and such conditions, things that are real come to look the way they do. The real and the apparent belong to one world, and to understand appearances is to understand how they arise in that world.

Hegel more than accepted Kant's belief that knowledge is not passive but active; he enlarged upon it and went beyond it. Unlike Kant, he insisted that knowledge is essentially the product of a plurality of minds. The ideas used to acquire a coherent image of a world do not arise separately in each particular mind; they are essentially public. They form a system of ideas which is a joint product and a common inheritance. Nor does the system remain unchanged; it develops from age to age in the course of history. Hegel saw knowledge, as Kant did not, as a product of human intercourse and of history; but in making this comparison between Hegel and Kant, I do not suggest that Kant, if he had been challenged, would have said anything so absurd as that every man acquires his view of the world separately from every other, and that all their views are alike only because they have the same organs of sense and use the same basic ideas. I say only that Kant, in developing his theory of knowledge, took almost no account of human intercourse and history, whereas Hegel took large account of them. For example, he insisted that self-knowledge and knowledge of others grow together, that how a man sees himself depends on how others see him and how he sees them. He also took notice of the fact that language, the system of concepts that men use to describe and to explain things and events, is a product of man's dealings with his fellows.

The extent to which Hegel saw knowledge as a product of human intercourse has been less recognized than it might have been because of his metaphysics. He conceived of reality as a process whereby 'Infinite Mind' or 'Spirit' reveals itself to itself, realizes its essence, becomes actually what it is potentially, and acquires self-knowledge by projecting itself as a world which it begins by taking as external to, and independent of, itself and comes at last to recognize as its own product. This conception of reality is bold but obscure, and is unacceptable (so it has been argued) even on purely logical grounds. But the merits of this conception are not our concern. The point that I now want to make is that Hegel thought of this 'Infinite Spirit' as revealed in the totality of things, and therefore also in the achievements, social and cultural, of mankind. Indeed, he thought of it as revealed at its higher levels, at the levels of consciousness and reason, in these achievements, and it is with these levels that we are now concerned. Spirit, as Hegel conceived of it, is not something that exists apart from the course of events and activities that reveal its essence; it does not stand to its manifestations as a cause to its effects. It is not an unknowable reality behind a known world of appearances. To understand how appearances come to be as they are is to know reality for what it is. Spirit, at the levels of consciousness and reason, is not a power outside men impelling them to behave as they do; at these levels, it exists only in their social and cultural achievements. Its achievements are their achievements, and their achievements are essentially those of social beings involved in a course of change. To know reality is to understand the process whereby Spirit reveals itself; and to understand the process is to understand the place of every stage in it, how from each stage its successor emerges, and how all the stages together constitute the progress of Spirit, its becoming actually what it is potentially. Conversely, fully to understand any part or stage of the process is to understand how it necessarily has just *that* place in the process.

Spirit moves progressively towards self-knowledge—or, in other words, towards an understanding of the world (both the 'natural' world and the world of culture, the distinctively human world) as a revelation of itself. Therefore, since Spirit, at the level of consciousness and reason, is revealed in the achievements of mankind, in the world of culture, it follows that mankind also move progressively towards a full understanding of the world and their place in it. At earlier stages of man's progress men have illusions about nature, about society and about man. At later stages they come to understand these illusions for what they are. What is more, they come to understand how the illusions arose necessarily when they did and how later they were necessarily discarded. The understanding of the process of social and cultural change, a process that consists of the activities of the beings involved in it, grows as the process continues. At the earlier stages, there is no awareness of a process. Men believe that their environment, the social part of it no less than the natural, is unchanging. They lack a sense of history; they take it for granted that their ancestors felt and thought and behaved as they do, and that their successors will be like them. Their understanding of themselves and their environment is inevitably defective and based on illusions, for they do not know that what they take to be unchanging changes necessarily. But later they come to know it; they come to recognize that there is a course of change in which they are involved, a process whereby the manner of their lives and therefore also themselves are transformed by their own activities.

Though Hegel speaks of the natural world, no less than the human, as a projection of Spirit, it is above all the human world, the world of culture, that interests him. His philosophy has added nothing to our understanding of nature and a great deal to our understanding of man and society. Spirit, at the level of consciousness and reason, is manifest in the activities of an essentially social and progressive being; that is to say, a being who behaves in the ways distinctive of his kind only when he lives with other beings of that kind and is educated by his dealings with them. The world of culture, the world in which man behaves in distinctively human ways, not only consists of human activities but is also their product. How that world changes is determined by what it is: out of one social order, one culture, another is born.

So we have at the centre of Hegel's philosophy the conception of history as a process whereby mankind are educated by their own endeavours, so that the potential in men is made actual, and the experience of a self-conscious and reflective being leads to self-knowledge and self-mastery. Just as Spirit realizes its potentialities in a world which it comes gradually to recognize as the world of its own activities, as a projection of itself, so man educates himself, learns to behave in distinctively human ways, through activities which constitute a social and a moral order, a world of culture. Only in this world can man behave as a self-conscious and rational being. There could be no social and moral order, no world of culture, unless there were potentially self-conscious and rational beings, but equally such beings could not behave in the ways peculiar to their kind if they did not (or had not) lived in such a world. And just as Spirit, in projecting itself as a world, is at first not aware that it does so, so mankind to begin with do not know that the social and moral order, the world of culture, in which men have their being as men, is their own product.

Hegel distinguishes, at every stage of the process in which Spirit reveals itself, Spirit as it appears to itself at that stage from Spirit as it really is—or, alternatively, men as they appear to themselves from men as they really are. He distinguishes, in his own idiom, Spirit as it is *for itself* from Spirit as it is *in itself*, and thinks of it as moving by stages towards a condition in which what it is for itself coincides with what it is in itself: a condition in which all illusions are dispelled and Spirit knows itself for what it is. How Spirit appears to itself is not a mere effect of what it is, for it could not behave in the ways characteristic of a particular stage of its evolution unless at that stage it appeared to itself as it does. For example, the ancient Greeks could not have behaved as they did unless their conceptions of themselves and of the world, especially their social and cultural world, had been what they were.

Hegel did not speak, as Marx was to do, of 'social existence' and 'consciousness', but he did speak of 'Objective' and 'Subjective Spirit'. Objective Spirit consists of social rules, institutions and conventional modes of behaviour to which men are required or expected to conform; Subjective Spirit consists in ways of thinking and feeling, in attitudes of mind. Subjective and Objective Spirit affect one another, and neither could subsist without the other. Obviously, if men are to be able to live in society together, if there are to be enduring relations between them, if they are to be able to form intentions and carry them out, there must be a considerable measure of harmony between

Subjective and Objective Spirit. But the men who, at any time or place, behave in conventional ways may not see how these ways fit together to form a social order. Their beliefs about them may not concern them alone but more besides, some of it sheer fantasy, and may serve rather to express their hopes and fears than to explain the facts. Their beliefs and attitudes may to some extent conflict with established modes of behaviour. Indeed, Hegel says, not that they may, but that they must. Spirit, at the level of consciousness and reason, is both active and reflective. In other words, its progress is dialectical: tensions or 'contradictions' arise between different aspects of it, and their resolution, which is a work of the Spirit, carries it forward to a higher level and a fuller revelation of its essence, taking it nearer to self-knowledge and self-possession, when it is *for* itself what it is *in* itself. Or, if we abandon all talk of Spirit and speak only of mankind, we say: the progress of humanity is dialectical, tensions arise between different aspects of men's activities, and their resolution, which is a human achievement, carries mankind to a higher level, one that brings men closer to a full understanding and mastery of their environment, especially that part of it which consists of their own social activities.

Man, society, history

Even if we reject Hegel's conception of reality as Infinite Spirit in process of realizing itself there are still ideas of his about man and society, and about the course of history, that we can accept: important ideas which to Hegel, but not to us, seem to be logically bound up with this conception. We can agree that essentially human capacities (those that distinguish man from other animals) are developed in men by their own activities; that these activities both constitute the social order and change it; that this is as true of primitive as of advanced societies, though men in primitive societies are not aware of it. We can also, though with reservations to be explained later, accept the distinction that Hegel makes between Objective and Subjective

Spirit, between conventional modes of behaviour on the one hand, and beliefs, sentiments and attitudes, on the other. Only self-conscious and rational beings can have conventions as distinct from mere habits, and they must have them if they are to develop the capacities peculiar to them. Conventional modes of behaviour are products of the same activities through which men acquire the ability to reason and to be objects of thought to themselves. Men can act rationally only because they can define their aims and pursue them deliberately, which they could not do if they had not the use of language, a social product; and in any case, many of their aims have no meaning except in the context of a social order. So Objective and Subjective Spirit, understood in this way, though they are distinguishable, necessarily go together; neither could exist in the absence of the other. Yet tensions can arise between them, and if they are to be resolved, the resolution must be the work of the very beings aspects of whose life they are. So, too, whether or not they take the form of theories, men's beliefs about the social order—or about the world in general—can be false or fantastic, and yet be closely bound up with that order, both when they justify and when they subvert it.

Hegel's distinction between Objective and Subjective Spirit corresponds to some extent to the distinction that Marx was to make later between social existence and consciousness. But the correspondence is far from complete. Hegel applies the word Spirit to both of the things he contrasts with one another; Spirit or Mind is manifest in institutions just as much as in the beliefs and sentiments of individuals. Institutions are merely conventional modes of behaviour, and conventional behaviour involves the use of ideas no less than other kinds of behaviour do. We can, no doubt, distinguish between what conventional behaviour signifies, what it is taken to mean, the beliefs and sentiments it expresses (which may or may not be sincere) from what a person really believes and feels when he behaves conventionally. We can also distinguish (and this is quite another distinction) between what conventional behaviour signifies and other beliefs and sentiments distinct from though affected by it. It may be that Hegel, when he contrasted Objective and Subjective Spirit, had both these distinctions vaguely in mind. The line he draws between these two aspects of Spirit is not precisely drawn, but he does at least, by the very terms he uses, make it clear that every kind of social activity involves 'consciousness'; that is to say, a kind of thinking possible only to beings that use ideas.

It would be unjust to Marx to suggest that he ever explicitly denied this. On the contrary, he sometimes came close to saying it and more often implied it. Yet the contrast he makes between social existence and consciousness is odd and misleading. Taken literally, it suggests that there are forms of social activity that do not involve the use of ideas. It is improbable that Marx ever intended to suggest this: to suggest that any kind of properly social activity can be merely instinctive and habitual. Certainly, the suggestion is inconsistent with his own idea of man as *essentially* a social being who develops the capacity to behave in specifically human ways only in social intercourse. And yet the distinction he made between social existence and consciousness does suggest that consciousness includes all mental operations that involve the use of ideas. He said, for example, that social existence determines consciousness but is not determined by it. Commentators disagree about what he meant here by the word 'determines', but the use of it seems to attribute some kind of primacy to social life over thought in whatever form. It is his belief in this primacy that is supposed, as much as anything, to set Marx apart from Hegel.

We could avoid some of the difficulties of Marx's position (and at the same time narrow the distance between him and Hegel) by so defining social existence that it excludes not all but only some kinds of thinking. We need not consider in detail how this could be done; it is enough, for our purpose, to concede that it could be. 'Social existence' would then consist of activities involving thought but excluding certain kinds of beliefs and sentiments: those that constitute 'consciousness' as distinct from 'social existence'. We might then claim for 'social existence' that it was *primary* or *fundamental* in relation to 'consciousness', affecting it in ways in which it was not affected by it, or affecting it to a much greater extent. Of course, if we did this, we should be putting ourselves to trouble that Marx avoided. Yet it might be trouble worth taking, even though, having taken it, we should find some Marxists quick to tell us that we were merely repeating what Marx had already said in fewer words. (To be accused of prolixity where Marx was concise would surely be the unkindest cut of all.)

Though Hegel says nothing of 'social existence' determining 'consciousness' and does not speak of 'ideology', the idea of the view or image of the world, the *Weltanschauung*, takes a large place in his philosophy. The ideas men use to describe the world and themselves in relation to it, and to express their feelings and attitudes, are not innate and unchanging but are products of human intercourse and of history. Or, rather, as Hegel sees it, they are products of Spirit at the levels at which it is manifest in the activities of finite rational beings. If, then, we discard the Hegelian conception of Spirit, what we are left with are the activities of such beings—or, rather, of men, the only such beings known to us. But ideas and institutions are not products of human activity in the way that tables and chairs, or even works of art, are so; they are not deliberately made for use nor deliberate attempts at self-expression. Or, at least, only some of them are, for, as we have seen, men must already have a system of ideas, a language, before they can invent ideas. A system of ideas is the undeliberate product of a community of persons, and it changes with time; though, of course, to any particular man, it is not his own product but a cultural inheritance which he acquires from others, and in any case he acquires only a part of it.

The understanding of how ideas and institutions arise, how they are related to one another, how they change, comes long after they have arisen. Only a being able to use ideas—that is to say, a rational being—can make descriptions and explanations, can form purposes and pursue them deliberately, putting some before others, and can be aware of itself as a rational being among other such beings, as a member of a community, as a part of a world. Only a rational being can have a *Weltanschauung*; and, indeed, always does have one, for there is always some conception of a world, of a scheme of things, implicit in a system of ideas, a language, and therefore also some conception of the place in that world of the being that uses the ideas. Whoever has ideas has a language, for ideas are useless—indeed, are not properly ideas—except as parts of a system. His language may be poor but still it is a system of ideas.

A *Weltanschauung* need not be a true image of the world, and the men that have it need not be able to describe it. It may be no more than implicit in their ways of speaking and in all their behaviour that involves thought. That is to say, they cannot be self-conscious and rational unless they can use ideas, which involves their having some such image, but they need not be able to give a true description of the image in order to be able to use ideas. Indeed, it is implicit in Hegel's philosophy—so at least it seems to me—that they cannot give a true description of the image until it is a true image. In other words, they cannot explain correctly how they conceive of the world until they conceive of it as it really is. Thus, if they philosophize, if they construct theories to explain the world and their theories are false, they have illusions, not only about the world, but also about their theories. If their understanding of the world is imperfect, so too is their understanding of the ideas they use to describe and explain it, and to act purposefully in it.

Hegel and also Marx, whose conception of ideology owes much to Hegel, believed that mankind make progress towards a full understanding of their environment and themselves, and therefore towards a condition in which they can form, in the light of this understanding, aims they can achieve. In the idiom of Hegel,

Spirit moves towards a condition in which it ceases to be opaque to itself, to have illusions about itself, to be estranged from itself, to frustrate itself. But the progress of Spirit is also, as Hegel conceived of it, a progress of man. And Marx, of course, spoke only of human progress. He saw mankind moving towards a condition in which men come at last to understand the social order and the world of culture which are the products of their past activities, of the course of history, and consist of their present ones. When at last they achieve this condition, they will achieve freedom; they will understand themselves, their aims and their environment. They are no longer frustrated by a social order of their own making which they yet do not understand or control, and are not victims of their own illusions about that order and themselves—of ideology in the sense of false consciousness. Their progress is *dialectical* because it takes the form of tensions or contradictions arising between different aspects of their lives which they alone can resolve, and whose resolution carries them forward towards the condition in which they are no longer frustrated and deceived by their own activities and ideas. It is dialectical because it involves self-frustration and self-deception and also the overcoming of them; because it comes of a capacity distinctive of their species, the capacity to use ideas and form purposes, which leads inevitably to their frustrating and deceiving themselves but ensures also that eventually they shake off these self-imposed burdens.

Hegel and Marx, the two thinkers to whom above all we owe the concept of ideology as we use it today, believed in a kind of progress that is dialectical, which each of them conceived in his own way. Nevertheless, the concept (or, more accurately, the family of concepts) as we now have it is not logically tied to this belief in progress. We can reject the belief and retain the concept. Indeed, the concept is indispensable, though we may use it under another name.

3/Thought and Its Social Conditions

Hegel, though he distinguished Objective from Subjective Spirit, never distinguished 'social existence' or social conditions from consciousness or thought, or ideas generally from ideology in the broadest sense of the word. It was Marx who, if he was not the first to make this distinction, was the first to make much of it, to insist on it as a key to the proper understanding of society and of man as a social being. Marx's assertion that social existence determines consciousness is perhaps the most often quoted of all, at least by sociologists. It is much more a favourite with them than the distinction he makes between the 'material substructure' of society and the 'ideological superstructure'. The sociologists of knowledge who study ideas, beliefs and theories in relation to the social conditions in which they arise or come to be widely used or accepted, are particularly impressed by it. Marx, as they (some of them, at least) see it, was never more happily inspired than when he uttered these words, even though he failed to see clearly their full import. For example, Karl Mannheim, in *Ideology and Utopia*, says that 'it was Marxist theory which first achieved a fusion of the particular and the total conceptions of ideology' (p. 66); and also that 'with the emergence of . . . the total conception of ideology, the simple theory of ideology develops into the sociology of knowledge' (p. 69). It is where Marxist theory contrasts 'consciousness' with 'social existence' that the 'total conception of ideology' emerges; it is there, if anywhere.

Marx and Mannheim

Now Marx, as we have seen, did not explain just what he meant by 'social existence' or by 'consciousness', nor just how he conceived of the relation between them. It is arguable that what Mannheim calls the 'total conception of ideology' does not emerge in his theory but has only been read into it. It is arguable that by social existence Marx meant only what he called the 'economic foundation' or 'material substructure' of society, though it is odd and misleading to use so broad a term to refer only to economic activities. It is also odd and confusing to say that social existence determines consciousness and not the other way about, and then to admit (as Marx quite often did, in so many words or by implication) that each affects the other. To say and to admit this is not necessarily to contradict oneself, but it calls for explanation. If one thing can determine another and not the other way about, and yet the two can interact, we want to be told just what kind of determining makes this possible.

Sometimes, when we say that A determines B, we mean that whatever happens to B is an effect of something that has happened to A; sometimes we mean that A sets limits to what can happen to B (or to what B can do), whereas B does not do the same to A; sometimes we mean that A affects B considerably more than B does A, or that A sets narrower limits for B than B does for A, thereby implying that these effects or these limits can be measured, at least roughly. And sometimes we have in mind, not a causal relationship, but one of another kind: we mean that A is a situation from which B has a determinate appearance for any observer at A. If, then, B is not a situation from which an observer can observe A, we have a sense of 'determine' that allows us to say that A determines B and is not determined by it. These are not, perhaps, the only senses of the word that are relevant but they are, I think, the most important. Which, then, did Marx have in mind when he said that social existence *determines* consciousness, or that the material substructure *determines* the ideological superstructure? In some contexts perhaps one, and in other contexts, another. The trouble is that the context too often affords us no clue. It is idle to speculate.

Let us consider, for a moment, what is involved in man's

being, in a way unique to his species, a social being. For that is what Marx and Mannheim say that he is; he acts, so they think, in typically human ways only when he acts as a social being, as a being whose capacities are developed by social intercourse. Now, other animals besides man keep enduring company together, living in packs or herds, and are affected by so doing. They acquire habits they would not otherwise have. Man, too, acquires habits as a result of living with his fellows. But he also acquires institutions or conventional modes of behaviour, and it is in the process of acquiring them that he becomes social in the way that he alone among animals is so. How, then, do conventional modes of behaviour differ from habits?

The man who acts conventionally recognizes a situation in which he is required or expected to behave in a certain way. He is capable of saying to himself: 'This is what is done in this sort of situation.' He is capable of defining a situation; he has some idea of a mode of behaviour that is normal in any situation of a given kind. Man is a social being, not by virtue of his habits, but by virtue of his conventions. This was not perhaps a commonplace among social theorists in Marx's time as it is today, but it is, I think, implicit in Marx's doctrine that man is essentially a social being. Conventional behaviour involves the use of ideas or the capacity to use them. For, though a man may come to act conventionally by habit, he must in the first place—if his behaviour is to be conventional and not merely habitual—have learned to behave that way by learning to define a situation as other people define it and to recognize what is required or expected of anyone in a situation of that kind.

Social conditions consist, presumably, of social relations, and these relations are defined in terms of conventional modes of behaviour. John is the husband of Mary if he behaves towards her in the ways required or expected of a husband, or if it is recognized that he has the right and the duty to do so. What, then, can be meant by saying that men's social conditions determine their ideas? We can, no doubt, distinguish social relations in terms of the ideas, the beliefs and the claims involved in the conventional modes of behaviour that define them. But, if we do that, we do no more than establish a correlation between social relations, on the one hand, and beliefs and claims, on the other. We do not explain the sense in which social relations determine ideas.

We can, if we like, speculate about how it was that men came, in the first place, to be *social* beings in a sense unique to their species; how conventions and ideas gradually arose among them. We can point to needs and to capacities peculiar to them depending on their physical set up—as, for example, on their erect stature, their hands, their brains, their jaws, which enabled them to become users and makers of tools and to acquire speech. Unless they had had these needs and capacities, they would never have become, in this unique sense, social beings. We may even say that, at a certain stage of the evolution of their species, they would not have survived, had they not become social beings.

Speculating in this way, we throw no light whatever on how social conditions are related to ideas; we do no more than suggest how they may both have arisen out of needs and capacities prior to them. We speak only (to use the idiom of Marx) of a physical substructure determining a social and ideological superstructure. Marx, on one or two occasions, and Engels more frequently, came close to doing just this. But these assumptions as to how the physical affects the social and ideological do not entail that the social affects the ideological in the same way. Indeed, it is pretty obvious that we have here two kinds of influence that differ greatly from one another. Man's physique changes very slowly whereas his social conditions and his ideas both change quickly. The sense in which the physical 'substructure' is prior to the 'social and ideological superstructure' is clear enough; it was the first to evolve and the superstructure could not exist without it. Though social conditions and ideas can vary greatly while the human physique remains unchanged, it is obvious that this 'substructure' sets limits to the forms that the 'superstructure' can take and is itself little affected by it. The sense in which the physical is *basic* in relation to the social and the ideological, and the sense in which it *determines* them are clear enough, difficult though it may be to define the exact limits that it sets to the forms they can take. But in just what sense does what is social determine what is ideological?

I suggested earlier that we could perhaps distinguish among social activities some that are primary from others that are secondary, and that we might use the word 'consciousness' or 'ideology' to refer only to the thinking involved in the secondary activities. Nobody, as far as I know, has ever succeeded in making such a distinction, though there have been several half-hearted attempts to make it. For example, Marx treated 'production' as a basic activity, but he never made it clear what was to be included in it. Are artists and thinkers who make a living by their work producers? But even if someone were to define a sense in which some activities were primary in relation to others, he might still find that neither category affected the other more than it was affected by it. He might also find that it was pointless to apply the word 'ideological' to the secondary rather than to the primary activities.

Now, it may be that those who say that social existence determines consciousness, or alternatively that social conditions determine thought, have in mind a connection between them different from, say, the connection between a fall in temperature and the turning of water into ice. They are perhaps thinking of something more like the connection between how an observer stands to an object he observes and how that object appears to him. For example, Mannheim speaks of a social situation and a social point of view, and this, after all, is a quite usual way of speaking. Quite often, if we want to explain how it is that someone comes to think as he does, we place him socially. He is, we may say, English, middle-class, Edwardian, an old Harrovian, the father of several children. Just as we can 'place' an individual in this way, so too we can 'place' a group; we can point to the social relations or social roles common to its members which distinguish them from the members of other groups. And when we attribute a point of view to an individual or a group we do more, presumably, than just assert a correlation between social relations or social roles, on the one hand, and beliefs and attitudes, on the other. We imply that, somehow, it makes sense for persons who stand in those relations, or who play those roles, to have these beliefs and attitudes.

When we 'place' an individual or a group socially, we do so within a social system; that is to say, within a system of social relations such that the persons between whom the relations subsist all belong to the same society. We can 'place' an Englishman or a group of Englishmen 'socially' in the English society of his or their day; but we cannot 'place' him or them in, say, Chinese society. Nor can we 'place' a social system 'socially', though we can point to the region where it flourishes or flourished, and to the period. If we take whatever we choose to call a social system, we cannot speak of a point of view or place common to all its members, for the simple reason that points of view or places are located within the system. How, then, if we speak broadly of 'consciousness' or 'thought', or of ideas and beliefs taken generally, can we say that it or they are 'relative to' or 'dependent on' a point of view? We can, no doubt, compare one social system with another; we can explain how the social relations and ideas that belong to it arose; we can explain, too, how eventually it was replaced by another. We can do it, provided we can make up our minds just what social relations and ideas constitute it, provided we can identify it. But if we do this, we do not define a social place or point of view common to all who are members of the same society; we merely explain how the society, within which individuals and groups have different points of view, differs from other societies or how it came into existence.

We all know what it is to have a point of view in the physical world. It may take a philosopher to explain what is involved logically in the conception of a world in which observers who move from place to place can distinguish changes in the way that things appear to them from changes in things as they are in themselves. But we all recognize what it is for an observer to have a place in such a world and to observe what falls within his range of vision from a given point of view. We see that it makes sense to speak of an observer having a place and a point of view only within the context of a stable world. We see also that we cannot intelligibly speak of a point of view common to all observers in that world—unless we think of them as observers of some other world so distant from their own that their different places in their own world make no perceptible differences to how the other world appears to them. These observers could not conceive of a world in which they had different and changing points of view if they had only ideas whose meanings varied with the points of view. Indeed, the very notion of such ideas is absurd. It is appearances that are relative to the point of view of the observer, changing as his point of view changes, and not the ideas he uses to describe them or to define his point of view. Unless this were so, he could have no conception of what an appearance or a point of view was.

The idea of a social point of view is more elusive. If we think of a society as not changing, and of an individual or group changing his or its 'place' in it, we have something analogous to a change in physical position and point of view. The 'places' that individuals and groups could occupy remain the same—that is implied by saying that the society has not changed—though individuals and groups can change their places, ceasing to stand in some social relations and coming to stand in others. But if the society changes, this is so no longer. There is then a change in the system and not just a change of places within it. It then becomes more difficult to decide what one means by changes in 'social points of view', for the system within which the points are located is no longer the same.

We have seen that observers in a physical world, having different and changing points of view inside it, not only *can* but *must* have ideas about it that do not change with their points of view, if they are to be aware of themselves as observers. They must also, if they are to be able to communicate with one another, share the same ideas. Indeed, Marx and Mannheim and others who have spoken of social conditions as determining ideas all agree that ideas are essentially public, that men come to have them in the process of learning to communicate with one another. Their different and changing points of view do not prevent their all using the same ideas to describe and explain things and events in the physical world. So too, presumably, their different and changing places in the social world do not prevent their using the same ideas to describe and explain their own and one another's behaviour. Their ideas cannot be 'relative' to their social points of view, for the ideas are shared but not the points of view. Just as observers in the physical world could not be aware that they all belonged to one world in which their points of view differ and change unless they shared ideas about that world, unless they understood it in the same way no matter what their points of view, so too the members of a society could not be aware that they belonged to it, and could not sustain their roles inside it, unless they shared ideas about it, unless their understanding of their own and other people's places in society were not relative to their own places. Understanding necessarily requires that ideas be not relative to points of view, whether the 'points of view' are physical or social.* On the other hand, if we define the sharing of a social point of view as the sharing of ideas, we argue in a circle.

---

*Mannheim, I suspect, failed to see this. He wrote: 'Controversy concerning visually perceived objects (which . . . can be viewed only in perspective) is not settled by setting up a non-perspectivistic view (which is impossible). It is settled by understanding, *in the light of one's own positionally determined vision*, why the object appeared differently to one in a different position. Likewise, in our field also, *objectivity is brought about by the translation of one perspective* into the terms of another.' *Ideology and Utopia*, pp. 270–1 (my italics). This talk of 'translating' one perspective into 'the terms' of another really makes no sense.

Those who say that *all* ideas and beliefs are socially determined or are 'relative' to the social conditions of the persons who use or hold them never stick for long to this extreme position. They always from time to time retreat from it, though they often return to it as soon as the uneasiness that moved them to retreat is dissipated. They are attracted to it and yet feel insecure in it. They hold to it fitfully, as if they were not quite sure what they were letting themselves in for. So much so, indeed, that it is perhaps misleading to speak of an extreme position, as if there were only one. To say that all ideas and beliefs are socially determined may be equivalent to saying that they all are 'relative' to social situations, or it may not. What I have called an extreme position is, in fact, a range of positions that the writers attracted to them do not state clearly. I have confined myself to following up one or two of their suggestions.

Marxists attracted to the doctrine that ideas and beliefs are socially determined have for the most part thought it enough to repeat it without explaining just what they understood by it. They have not drawn from it the conclusion that all beliefs are true only for their own time. Following Marx and also Hegel, they have distinguished knowledge, understanding things as they really are, from what is taken for knowledge but is not so. They do not distinguish among theories some that are capable of reaching conclusions true under all social circumstances from others that are not. No doubt, they believe that in bourgeois society the social studies provide real knowledge much less than do the natural sciences. But this they think is a defect of bourgeois society. There is nothing about human behaviour that precludes the study of it ever becoming scientific—if 'scientific' is taken to mean using methods well adapted to discovering the truth. Marxists think of Marxism, which is concerned with human behaviour much more than with natural events, as being just as 'objective' in its own sphere as the natural sciences in theirs. The explanations it offers may come to be improved upon in the future, but this is true also of the explanations of the physicist. The social studies can, in principle, explain social phenomena and the course of social change as they really are and not just as they appear to people under such and such circumstances. And yet the Marxists who say that ideas and beliefs are socially determined claim to be saying something more than just that the creatures that have them are social beings and that there are social conditions of their having them. They claim to be saying more than what nobody has ever wanted to deny. Unfortunately, they do not explain what this something more is.

Mannheim, who believed that Marx failed to see the full implications of his own doctrine about social existence and consciousness, distinguished among the sciences—or perhaps I should say the systematic studies—some whose conclusions are (or can be) universally true from others whose conclusions at best are true only for people who look at what they study from 'the same point of view'. He did not always draw the line between the two at the same place. He seems to have held consistently that the conclusions of logic and mathematics, if correctly arrived at, are universally true. He was more equivocal, I think, about the natural sciences. (K. Mannheim, *Ideology and Utopia*: Compare what he says on p. 70 ff., with what he says on p. 244.) But about the social or human studies, though he was quite willing to call them sciences, he had few doubts: their conclusions, he thought, are true only for people who are similarly situated, who look at what they study from the same point of view. The situation, the point of view, is of course social.

Mannheim admitted that all ideas, even those of logic and mathematics, are social products in the obvious sense that only beings whose capacities are developed by social intercourse form and use them. He not only admitted but insisted upon it, as every sociologist of knowledge has done. The social theorist or the historian of ideas, provided he has access to the relevant facts, can explain the origins of logic and mathematics, just as the psychologist (for example, Jean Piaget) can explain how a child learns to count or to distinguish false from true statements. Nor did Mannheim deny that even the foundations of logic and mathematics change, that the logician of our day makes basic assumptions unknown to Aristotle and the geometer starts from definitions unknown to Euclid. Clearly, the truths of logic and mathematics are not universal in the sense that logicians and mathematicians have accepted them in all societies. And there are, no doubt, social conditions of their emergence. The historian can explain why geometry developed among the Greeks as it never did among the Egyptians, just as he can explain why the empirical sciences made relatively little progress in ancient Greece.

There is implicit in Mannheim's distinction between knowledge that is socially relative and knowledge that is not another distinction between the *social conditions* of knowledge and the *social perspective* that determines its contents. For example, the West Europeans, unless they had acquired certain skills and had had certain opportunities and incentives, would not have made, in the last three or four centuries, the immense progress they have made in the natural and the formal sciences. The historian, if only he can get at the relevant facts, can explain how it was that they acquired these skills and came to have these opportunities and incentives; he can point to the social conditions which favoured their doing so. But these conditions are not a social situation or point of view that determines the contents of the natural and formal sciences. It is at least conceivable that different social conditions might have provided the same opportunities and incentives and encouraged the same skills, and that the sciences, natural and formal, would have developed much as they did. There are social conditions that favour or impede the growth of any branch of knowledge, but the contents of only some branches depend on the social situation or point of view of the knower. Mannheim does not make this distinction between branches of knowledge in quite the way I have made it, but it is, I think, implicit in some of his arguments.

The distinction seems to me untenable, and I shall try to explain why later. But before I do that, I must point out that those who make the distinction, overtly or by implication, sometimes deny that they are thereby committed to holding that progress is impossible in the studies whose contents depend on the social point of view. Mannheim, for one, denied it. As literacy spreads, as the number of students increases, as society devotes more and more of its resources to encouraging them, all branches of study make progress. The social studies, not less than the others, respond to favourable circumstances; they too give a return on resources, financial and intellectual, invested in them. Some societies understand themselves from their 'point of view' much better than others do from theirs; they collect and classify vastly more information, and produce more comprehensive and sophisticated theories to explain the facts. So, too, some societies go much further than others do in studying other societies. For example, social anthropologists trained in the West have spent a great deal of money and time studying 'primitive' peoples who have spent not a penny nor a minute studying western peoples—at least not until after they have been to some extent 'westernized' and have acquired a different 'point of view'. Mannheim would not, I am sure, have denied that some peoples understand other peoples better than these others understand them. Their understanding, presumably, is from their own point of view. But what if they study (as, of course, they do) the behaviour and beliefs of other peoples who themselves make no such studies? Do they understand this behaviour and these beliefs better than do the people whose behaviour and beliefs they are? Do they understand these people's 'point of view' better than they understand it themselves? Would Mannheim have denied it? Or would he perhaps have admitted that, say, a social anthropologist from the West is better equipped intellectually to understand even the point of view of illiterate tribesmen than they are themselves, and yet have insisted that he can understand it only from his own western point of view?

In the regions inhabited by primitive peoples, there are not only men but wild animals peculiar to those regions. The western zoologist who studies them uses ideas conceived in the West. Zoology is a natural science; there are social conditions of its emergence and flourishing. But not, apparently—so Mannheim would imply, at least sometimes—a 'social point of view' to which it is relative. Zoology, in this respect, differs from social anthropology. Why should this be so?—Or, rather, why should anyone think it is so?

'Relativity' of ideas and beliefs

I have not been concerned with the views of Marx and Mannheim for their own sake but only as examples of a certain way of thinking. Their views have been interpreted in widely different ways. This is especially true of Marx, though Mannheim, too, has had both defenders and critics. I am sure that my brief account of what Marx meant or may have meant when he said that social existence determines consciousness would be dismissed by some of his admirers, and even critics, as superficial or perverse. My own belief is that Marx, like Mannheim, vacillated between several different positions without being aware how they differed. I have discussed some of these positions briefly only to help me make some points I wanted to make. I want now to consider one or two questions more generally, with no more than passing reference to the views of particular thinkers.

I have said that though social theorists sometimes write as if *all* ideas were determined by social conditions or relations in a way that suggests that there is a sphere of social life which does not involve the use of ideas, they soon retreat from this position whenever they have to face up to its implications. No doubt, ideas do arise in a social context, and any full account of their emergence must point to social conditions. But the same is true of social relations or institutions. If to be 'socially determined' is to arise only under determinate social conditions, then all, or nearly all, social relations are socially determined. I say *nearly all* and not *all* because, if we accept the Darwinian rather than the Mosaic account of the origin of our species, we must suppose that there was a time when men were not socially related as they alone now are, just as we must suppose that there was a time when they did not use ideas. Whatever moved them in the first place to become social beings, to acquire ideas and to behave conventionally, was clearly not a social cause.

I suggested also that we could perhaps, if we thought it worth while, distinguish the use of ideas actually involved in the forms of conventional behaviour that constitute having social relations from other uses of them. No doubt, there are many ideas that are used both in such behaviour and outside it. Nevertheless, if we did make this distinction between two uses of ideas, we could then enquire how social relations, or conventional modes of behaviour, affect the use of ideas outside them. We could, for example, enquire how they affect the making of different kinds of theories—theories about natural phenomena, or about abstract ideas and their implications, or about how men behave or ought to behave. We could also enquire how they affect art and religious beliefs. All these things are deeply affected by social relations and conventional modes of behaviour, and in turn, no doubt, deeply affect them.

But though this, in principle, could be done, it is worth noticing that nobody has ever tried to do it. Neither Marx nor any disciple of his has, so far as I know, engaged in any such enquiry. No doubt, social theorists and historians, both Marxists and others, often ask how social conditions affect ideas. But by social conditions they do not mean just social relations (including the ideas involved in them); they mean any social relations and ideas which to them seem relevant. They mean the social relations and ideas current in the place and time when the change in ideas or attitudes that they want to explain occurred. That is to say, what they mean includes both 'social existence' and 'consciousness', and they do not go to the unnecessary trouble of distinguishing between them. For their aim is not to produce evidence in support of Marx's aphorism but to explain how certain beliefs or attitudes arose or disappeared. And the ideas whose emergence or decay they seek to explain are quite often ideas involved in social relations. In other words, quite often, when, for example, they say they are enquiring how ideas about marriage or property changed, they are much more concerned to explain how these institutions changed than how beliefs or theories about them did so. No doubt, social conditions do determine men's ideas, but then social conditions also determine all social relations, except those whose emergence coincided with the earliest use of ideas. They determine them in at least the sense that they set limits to how they can change. Is this all that is meant by the many people who say that social conditions determine men's ideas? I suspect that very often it is, though they are themselves under the impression that they are saying something much less obvious, much more profound: something that the more modest of them believe they could never have thought of for themselves but which they accept gratefully on good authority.

We have seen that the assertion that social conditions determine ideas is sometimes the first step in an argument which concludes that knowledge is relative to the point of view of the knower. We have seen, too, that this conclusion is never left unqualified. Exceptions are always made for some branches of knowledge—at least for the formal sciences, if not for the natural sciences as well. But, we may ask, why make any exceptions? Or, if some are made, why not abandon the conclusion altogether? Why not admit that, in every sphere, there can be knowledge that is not 'relative' in this sense? Everyone admits that every kind of idea and every branch of knowledge has its social origins. Why, then, exempt any ideas, any branch of knowledge, from this relativity? Even the ideas of logic and mathematics are not universal. Indeed, some of them are the most abstruse of all.

The exemption in favour of the formal sciences is due, presumably, to the belief that there are some ideas indispensable to any coherent discourse, or to any language used to describe and to explain events, whatever their kind. It comes also of recognizing that ideas are required to explain the use and limitations of ideas. People who do not consider how ideas are used but merely use them know nothing of these other ideas, but anyone who thinks about thought and speech must use them. There are, thus, some ideas to be found in any language and others that are needed to explain the nature of language. Therefore the formal sciences, which study these ideas and their implications, are not relative to any social point of view, though some of the ideas they use or study are unfamiliar to most people, and some of their theories are so recondite that only a handful of people in the world understand them.

The empirical sciences must, however, use other ideas besides those that are independent of any particular kind of rational experience because they are involved in all kinds, or else in explaining what it is to have such an experience. Rational beings with different organs of sense from ours, different biological needs and different physical capacities, would receive sense impressions different from ours, would have different problems and different skills. They would use different ideas and have different 'world-images'. If they took to systematic empirical studies, they would put forward different hypotheses and construct different theories. The contents both of their everyday thinking about the natural world and of their natural sciences would be different. But would their ideas about scientific method, about the functions of hypotheses and theories, necessarily be different from ours? I mean so different from ours that we could never come to understand them? I see no reason why this should be so. After all, our ideas about scientific method, about how to reach valid conclusions in the empirical sciences, are not the same as those of our ancestors. We can explain how human ideas have changed; we can understand what they once were and what they have now become. Why should not the ideas we use to explain how human ideas about scientific method have changed enable us to explain how our ideas about it differ from those of rational beings physically different from ourselves? Our ideas about the empirical method do not depend logically on the internal properties of our sense impressions.

Two physically different species of rational beings, provided they could observe one another's behaviour sufficiently to recognize it as the behaviour of rational beings, could learn in time to communicate with one another. Each could discover how the experience, the 'image of the world', of the other differed from its own. They could not, of course, describe sensible qualities imperceptible to themselves, but they could construct an elaborate, though necessarily to some extent 'colourless', image of the world as it appeared to members of the other species. Each species could explain to the other its theories about the nature of the other's experience, and each species could correct or corroborate the theories of the other. The two species could learn in time to recognize the limits of communication between them.

I need not pursue this line of argument further. After all, the theorists who speak of the relativity of thought are concerned with the thought of only one species of rational being. What they have in mind is not, if I may so put it, 'physically or biologically relative' but 'socially relative' thought. Still, it is worth noticing that biologically different species able to think conceptually, to acquire languages, could go a long way towards understanding one another.

It is thought about human behaviour, both at the level of ordinary discourse and of 'science' and theory, that believers in the relativity of thought are really concerned about. This is the kind of thinking that they claim is inevitably 'relative' and therefore valid or true only under certain social conditions. Even when they claim more than this, when they say that thought about natural phenomena is 'relative', they do so only because it seems to them that the arguments they have used to prove the relativity of thought about human behaviour commit them to doing so. For example, Engels sometimes spoke as if natural science could be bourgeois, and other Marxists have done so too; but they have done it ambiguously and almost as an after-thought. Their heart has never been in it. What they have really wanted to say is that bourgeois thinkers, just because they are bourgeois, just because of their place in society, have an inade-quate and distorted image of how society functions and develops. It is true that they have exempted proletarian thinkers from the myopia and other defects of vision that afflict the bourgeois (for reasons which not everyone finds convincing). But their explana-tion of the deficiencies of bourgeois thinkers is not merely that their methods are inappropriate, that they lack relevant infor-mation or the concepts that would enable them to put the really illuminating questions. They do not find bourgeois thought de-fective for the sort of reasons that a historian of science might give for the deficiencies of Ptolemaic as compared with Coper-nican astronomy. The methods of bourgeois thinkers may be inappropriate and their concepts inadequate, but they cling to these methods and concepts because they are bourgeois—be-cause, though they do not know it, it suits them to think of society and social change in the way they do.

Critics of the Marxists—Mannheim among others—have argued that this exemption of Marxism (or of the 'proletarian consciousness' which, in Marxist eyes, amounts to much the same thing) is inconsistent with their own doctrine that social existence determines consciousness. According to Mannheim, Marx, by claiming for his own theory a privilege he denied to others, showed that he did not fully understand why it is that thought about human behaviour is necessarily 'relative'. He came close to understanding it, as some of his utterances show, but he did not get to the heart of it.

I shall not enquire why Mannheim believed that thought about human behaviour (not to speak of other things) is neces-sarily relative. Justice to him would require a much fuller con-sideration of his arguments than I can fit into the limits of this book. I shall enquire more generally: What is it about human behaviour and reflection upon it that has moved people to say this? Are they at all justified in saying it? The belief that ideas and theories about human behaviour are necessarily 'relative' is, after all, a fairly recent belief. We can find hardly a trace of it before the eighteenth century, and not much of it before the nineteenth. It is a belief that has spread with the study of history, especially social history and the history of ideas. But the other studies, the formal and natural sciences, also have their histories, no less than the study of human behaviour. All the sciences and studies are themselves forms of social behaviour, a kind of behaviour that changes perpetually in all its forms.

Science or systematic study, no matter what its sphere, always begins by using ideas in common use. It refines upon them and adds to them, and so acquires a special vocabulary of its own. These special vocabularies, though they in their turn affect common speech considerably, remain distinct from it and often grow more and more remote. All the sciences, all the systematic studies, formal, natural and human, are alike in this. In a quite obvious sense, all theory derives from practice and reacts upon it.

Nevertheless, there are important respects in which thought about human behaviour, both at the level of theory and of ordinary discourse, differs from thought about natural events. Human behaviour changes in character over time, and does so largely as the result of the influence of human thought upon it. This is not just a case of theory affecting practice; it is a case rather of thought affecting its object. For man, even when he is not engaged in theorizing, in systematic explanation, is something more than merely practical: he is also reflective and critical. Even when he is not a theorist, he does more thinking than is actually involved in the productive activity or social role he is engaged in. He also thinks and talks about this activity or role when he is not engaged in it. He does so even in illiterate societies where there is none of the systematic thinking that we call theory. This reflection upon an activity, which is distinct from the use of ideas involved in carrying it on, can deeply affect it.

Thus, thought about human behaviour affects it as thought about natural events does not affect them. Of course, how men think about natural events affects human behaviour, affects the social environment, but it does not affect the natural environment; or, rather, affects it much less and in quite different ways.

Again, both human behaviour and reflection upon it express, overtly or implicitly, the ideas men have as to what is desirable or right or admirable, or the reverse. These ideas or 'values' differ widely from place to place and from time to time. And so it is often said that reflection and theory about human behaviour are no more 'value-free' than the behaviour which is their object. No doubt, reflection and theory about natural events also have some purpose behind them, and men's purposes are affected by their values. But natural events do not themselves express these values, nor do descriptions and explanations of them do so, except to the extent that men attribute to natural objects, plants and other animals, properties they do not possess; desires, intentions and attitudes like their own. Human thinking about what is not human begins by being anthropomorphic but grows progressively less so as men's understanding of it and of themselves increases. It becomes more and more 'value-free' in a way that human thinking about human behaviour does not.

These peculiarities of thought, reflective and theoretical, about things human do, of course, make it more difficult for such thought to be 'objective' and 'value-free'. But I see no reason why they should make it impossible. Thought is objective where there are definite, consistent and relevant criteria of truth or probability which it satisfies; it is value-free when it describes or explains without passing value judgements, overtly or covertly. Thought about human behaviour, merely because this behaviour is purposeful and is often affected by how men think about it, and often gives effect or expression to judgements of value, is not thereby precluded from being objective and value-free.

To say that thought, when it is about human behaviour,

3—20 pp.

affects its object can be misleading. It is not strictly true. The thought in question, clearly, is not the thinking that forms part of the behaviour, by virtue of which it is *that* sort of behaviour. For to say that the thought that forms part of an action affects it is like saying that the shape of something affects it. The thought that affects human behaviour is external to the behaviour it affects. No doubt, a man who knows that he is being watched will not behave as he would have done had he not known it. But this is not a case of knowledge affecting its object, for its object is not his behaviour but his being watched. If he were not being watched but believed that he was, this false belief would affect his behaviour in just the same way. So, too, a man who 'watches himself behaving' is apt to behave differently. But here also, strictly speaking, the behaviour affected by the watching is subsequent to it. And, in any case, a great deal of human behaviour can be observed without its subjects being aware that it is; and again, a man can call to mind how he behaved when he was not 'watching' himself doing so. Just as we can study men behaving unobserved or unself-consciously, so we can study them behaving under observation and self-consciously.

Those who say that beliefs about human behaviour are 'relative' mostly do not go on to say that we cannot discriminate between them in respect of their truth or probability. They do not deny that there are criteria of truth that apply to them; they merely say that these criteria differ from one type of society to another. No doubt they do, to some extent. But we have to ask: How do they differ, and what conclusions are we to draw from their doing so? Did the Chinese, before their country was opened to western influences, or did the ancient Greeks apply different criteria from ours for assessing the truth of ordinary, non-theoretical, statements about human behaviour? It may be that a Chinese or an ancient Greek, if he were the sort of person who goes in for definitions, would define his criteria differently from the way that an Englishman similarly inclined would define his. But would this not apply equally to their criteria for assessing the truth of ordinary statements about natural events? All their definitions, Chinese, Greek or English, might be defective, and correct definitions of the criteria they in fact applied might show that they were pretty much alike.

At the level of theory, and not just ordinary discourse, their criteria might differ considerably more: that is to say, correct definitions of them might show that they did. But this, presumably, would apply as much to theories about natural events as to theories about human behaviour. Nobody denies that the natural sciences have made progress, and they have done so largely by acquiring more rigorous methods and more precise criteria and concepts enabling them to explain more and more of the phenomena they study clearly and economically. The social studies have made less progress in these ways than the natural sciences have, but then some of the natural sciences have made less progress than others.

The fact that human behaviour differs considerably from place to place and from age to age does not preclude us from distinguishing the ways in which it differs or changes from the ways in which it does not. It does not prevent us from acquiring ideas we can use to describe the respects in which it is similar everywhere, or over large areas for long periods, and the respects in which it is not. No doubt, the ideas in everyday use in any society or age are not well-adapted to this purpose. If we want to widen our understanding of human behaviour, if we want to think more clearly and consistently about it, we have often to weaken the hold on us of ideas in everyday use. But this is in no way peculiar to the human sciences; it applies equally to the natural and the formal ones. The ideas of the scientist, and even of the historian are cousins, at one or more removes, to the ideas of ordinary discourse. As Pascal saw three centuries ago, we find it difficult to think systematically, rigorously and economically, difficult even to use the ideas we ourselves construct to enable us to do so, because the hold on us of ordinary ways of thinking is so strong. And though it is more difficult, perhaps, for the student of human behaviour than for the natural scientist, it is possible and worth trying.

Marriage is different in England in our day from what it was in Greece in Aristotle's time. The Englishman who thinks of marriage is apt to think of it as he finds it in his own country and time; and this means that, unless he is careful, he is likely to misunderstand marriage as it was in Greece twenty-three centuries ago. But if he learns to use ideas which enable him to explain how far marriage in England today differs from marriage in ancient Greece and how far it is the same, it is absurd to say that he cannot help but use these ideas 'from an English point of view'. It is absurd to say it even if his explanation of Greek marriage is mistaken. To the extent that his account of Greek marriage differs from his account of English marriage he is not describing a Greek institution as if it were English. He may, in his account of ancient Greek marriage, use ideas unknown to the ancient Greeks and these may be ideas produced in England in the twentieth century. His use of them may even enable him to make true statements about Greek marriage which Aristotle himself, for lack of them, could not have made.

What can be meant by saying that an Englishman 'understands' Greek marriage from 'an English point of view'? Clearly, it must mean something more than that he is an Englishman who does the understanding. If he had blue eyes, we should not say that he understood Greek marriage from the point of view of a blue-eyed man. His understanding it from an 'English point of view' must mean, at the very least, his understanding (or misunderstanding) it as he would not do if he were not English. What it cannot mean is his understanding it, or some aspect of it, not as it really was, but only as it appears to him. Either he understands it or he misunderstands it. To say that he 'understands' it as he would not do if he were not English is to say that he uses ideas to explain it that he would not use if he were not English. These, presumably, would be ideas current only in England or for some reason more attractive to Englishmen than to others. Such ideas might be either a help or a hindrance to understanding Greek marriage. Their being English ideas does not ensure that they are either the one or the other. Nor does it mean that they are ideas that none but the English can use. If they are good ideas, if they are a help to understanding Greek marriage, then classical scholars in France and Germany would do well to adopt them. If they are bad ideas, if they are a hindrance, then classical scholars in England would do well to discard them. Their being ideas that first arose in the minds of Englishmen reflecting on marriage in England does not mean that they are forever beyond the reach of Germans and Frenchmen or that Englishmen, even married ones, writing about marriage in ancient Greece cannot help but use them—that they are stuck with them, like poor Mr Dick with the image of King Charles's head.

Human behaviour often expresses, though not always in words, the 'values' of the persons whose behaviour it is. In that case, it cannot be explained without reference to those values. But this does not mean that the explanation cannot be 'value-free'; that it cannot be merely descriptive and explanatory with no value judgement, express or implied, about it. The explainer, no doubt, has his own purposes in making the explanation, and his own values in forming those purposes; but he would have them also if he were explaining, not human behaviour, but natural events. It may well be that men, especially when they have passed the stage when they ascribe human qualities to natural objects, are much more often diverted from the pursuit of truth when they explain human behaviour than when they explain natural events. But this means only that it is more difficult to be objective about human behaviour. Which nobody doubts.

It is probable that people who say that descriptions and explanations of human behaviour are never 'value-free' do not mean to be taken quite literally. 'James and Anne got married on September 1st' looks, on the face of it, just as purely descriptive as 'There was a sharp frost on November 6th'. The second statement, no less than the first, could conceivably be made with the intention of proving someone to be a liar, but that would not make it a value judgement. Perhaps the people who say this have in mind only statements that ascribe motives, intentions, tastes and attitudes. Words used to refer to these 'states of mind' are often both descriptive and evaluative. But this does not mean that they can never be used for the first purpose without also being used for the second. Some words, according to the dictionary, have as many as thirty meanings, which is not to say that they are used in all of them every time they are used. If a word has several meanings, some descriptive and some evaluative, and yet need not—and indeed cannot—be used in all of them at once, why should it be impossible to use it in a descriptive sense without also using it to make a value judgement? But let that pass. Even if it were true that no word used to make value judgements could ever be used merely to describe or explain, it would not follow that the descriptions and explanations that contain it were not 'objective' or were true only 'from the point of view' of the person who makes them and others who share his values. Machiavelli approved of the politic lie, Savonarola perhaps did not. The sentence 'Lorenzo was a liar' is both descriptive and evaluative, and the descriptive part of it, if true, is no less true than the statement 'Florence is in Italy', and has the same meaning for Machiavelli and Savonarola.

The notion of 'total ideology'—that in general ideas and beliefs are 'relative' to the social situations or points of view of the people who have them, and are intelligible or true only 'for' them—is untenable. So, too, is the notion that ideas and beliefs that concern specifically human behaviour are so.

There is, of course, an important distinction to be made between two functions of beliefs and theories. They serve to describe and to explain, and they serve also to justify and encourage behaviour, or to condemn and discourage it, or to express hopes and other feelings, or to allay fears. The first function is often called *descriptive* and the second *persuasive*. Clearly, the same beliefs or theories can serve both functions—which makes it only the more important to distinguish between them. Beliefs and theories that are against the evidence or are unverifiable or are not examined critically do come to be accepted, often widely and ardently, because they are persuasive. The enquiry into how such beliefs and theories arise and come to be accepted in some communities or groups but not in others is an important part of the social and historical studies.

Ordinarily, when we speak of ideology, we have in mind persuasive theories and beliefs. But the word is not used to refer only to them. It is, as we have seen, used in several different senses, and often in contexts which do not make it clear what sense is being used. What is more, the social theorists whose ideas about it have been the most influential have failed to distinguish between these senses, or have taken it for granted that beliefs that are ideological in one sense are so in some other sense as well. For example, Marxists often speak of 'bourgeois ideology' as if it were both a set of persuasive beliefs and an image of society and social change as they necessarily appear to persons placed socially as the bourgeois are.

4/Ideology as Persuasive Belief and Theory

Persuasive Beliefs

A group of shipwrecked sailors, in danger of death in stormy seas, might believe, falsely or without good evidence, that help would come to them in time. Nobody would call such a belief ideological merely because the sailors clung to it to allay their fears. To be ideological a belief must be one that people resort to on most or many occasions of a given kind. But a belief like this ordinarily goes along with other beliefs. It belongs to a set of related beliefs to which a community or group resort in situations that recur quite frequently. The people who share these beliefs may acquire them gradually without even being aware that they form a more or less consistent set of beliefs. It might take a sociologist or a social anthropologist to explain how these beliefs are related to one another and to define the situations in which they are resorted to.

Often, a community or group share several distinct ideologies, each of them coherent enough in itself, some overlapping with others, which yet do not, taken together, form a system of beliefs that is a coherent whole. Ideologies to which people resort on different kinds of occasions need not be consistent with one another. It is not a condition of harmony, of the absence of disputes within the community or group or of 'tensions' within the minds of its members, that they should be. In a large and complex community, most people belong to several groups whose membership is not the same, so that any one person shares different ideologies with different people.

Ideology, thus conceived, is no less important in illiterate than in literate communities. Among both the illiterate and the literate, ideological beliefs are passed on from generation to

generation. This is done to a large extent deliberately; beliefs
are taught and not only acquired. The teachers, for the most
part, do not see themselves as persuaders—except in the sense
that every teacher is one. That is to say, they do not recognize
that the beliefs they teach are persuasive. This is clearly true of
teachers in primitive communities, for the very notion of a persuasive belief is unknown to them. But it is true also, as often as
not, of teachers in literate and sophisticated communities, where
this notion is widely familiar. In primitive communities, there
are few or no teachers by profession. In 'advanced' communities
there are many; and if the idea of persuasive beliefs is at all
familiar, it is apt to be most familiar among teachers and others
—journalists, writers, publishers—whose business is to provide
information and inculcate beliefs. Yet, even in the most sophisticated communities, the propagators of persuasive beliefs often
do not recognize that that is what they are.

Every teacher and publicist is, of course, a persuader and
knows that he is one. The physicist or biologist with no axe to
grind wants to persuade others of the truth of what he is saying.
Besides, there are times when he does have an axe to grind, as,
for example, when he wants to score off a rival or to achieve
something else for himself or for others. The political theorist or
the theologian may have exactly the same motives as the physicist for teaching what he does teach; he may be concerned primarily that others should share beliefs which he holds to be true,
or he may be keener to achieve something else. What makes
political theory and theology much more apt than physics or
biology to be ideological has nothing to do with the intentions
of the theorist or the theologian; it has to do only with the
motives and feelings of the persons who accept the beliefs and
with how they behave as a result of accepting them. If the beliefs
are accepted largely because they express or inhibit feelings, and
if they encourage or discourage some type of behaviour, not just
on a few occasions, but on all or most occasions of a given kind,
they are 'persuasive'. The propagator of the beliefs may or

3A

may not intend to arouse or inhibit feelings, to encourage or discourage behaviour, but he need not intend it for the beliefs to be 'persuasive' or ideological.

Again, beliefs are not always ideological (in the sense we are now discussing) when the propagator of them intends to influence feelings and behaviour. The man who calls out 'Fire' in a crowded theatre is not propagating an ideological belief, not even when he acts maliciously and there is no fire. For, as we have seen, an ideological belief is one that some community or social group* resort to on occasions of a given kind, and nearly always forms part of a set of such beliefs—though the set need not be a theory.

In advanced societies beliefs that are persuasive are mostly concerned with how people behave or ought to behave, or else are theological beliefs. A high proportion of them are incorporated into theories. Indeed, many first see the light of day in print. In primitive societies beliefs about natural events are also often ideological. This does not mean, of course, that we cannot distinguish, among the beliefs current in primitive societies, those that are ideological from those that are not. Primitive peoples, no less than advanced ones, need to give and to get true descriptions and explanations, both of natural events and human behaviour, and they assess the truth of them by using much the same criteria as are used in like circumstances by advanced peoples. They do not define the criteria, but then neither do most people in advanced societies—for most people are not logicians. Among all peoples, too, there are descriptions and explanations to which these criteria are not applied, or are applied loosely in a way that does not detract from their 'persuasiveness'.

In primitive societies, though there are both ideological and other beliefs, nobody distinguishes between them. In advanced societies, where some men at least reflect upon mental processes,

---

*At this stage, I refrain from qualifications and distinctions which I make later. An ideology which means little or nothing to most people in a community or group may mean a great deal to their leaders.

they distinguish between types of ideas and their uses, different kinds of beliefs and their effects. They distinguish the formal from the empirical sciences, and among the empirical sciences, the natural from the human or social ones. They also distinguish among the human studies, though with less assurance, the scientific from the historical: attempts to discover laws or, as some would put it, to establish hypotheses and to construct theories relating the laws and hypotheses to one another, from attempts to explain the behaviour of particular persons or groups of persons on particular occasions. They distinguish theology and mythology, accounts of beings and events not met with in ordinary experience or in scientific investigations, from science and history.

They distinguish, too, the use of ideas for descriptive and explanatory purposes from other uses of them; such uses as making requests and giving orders, making value judgements, expressing moods and feelings, and so on. Though the same speech or writing can combine several of these uses, the uses themselves can be distinguished; which does not mean, of course, that it is always easy to decide to what uses particular ideas are being put. Indeed, there are still large differences of opinion among philosophers and others as to how these different uses should be defined; differences that we, fortunately, need not consider. But we must at least take note of them, even though only in this summary fashion, if we are to understand what ideology, in the sense of persuasive belief, is.

We must notice, first of all, that ideology is overtly descriptive and explanatory. Sets of beliefs or theories that are ideological purport to tell us how things are or were, and how they come or came to be so. Rules and standards are not, in themselves, ideological, nor are value judgements. Nor, of course, are requests and commands, nor expressions of mood or feeling. Art, merely as such, is not ideological. Ideology is *primarily* 'persuasive' and is only, if I may so put it, *secondarily* 'prescriptive'. In that respect, it is like a fable by Aesop or La Fontaine; it is, on the face of it, a tale, though a tale that points a moral. If there were only the moral and not the tale, there would be no ideology; and it is always the tale that is put into words, and not always the moral. Besides, the teller of the tale may not wish to point a moral. What makes the tale ideological is that his audience, consciously or unconsciously, draws a moral from it.

The ideological tale need not be false, nor need it, strictly speaking, be a tale. It need not be mythology or history. It can purport to explain any action or event of a given kind; it can be science or pseudo-science. It can even be a general explanation of a kind that those who make or accept it admit is not scientific, though they claim that it is true.

Many sets of beliefs or theories that are ideological are also overtly prescriptive; they include injunctions and advice to men as to how they should behave, and they make value judgements. But the injunctions and advice, and the value judgements, are supported by assertions that purport to describe or explain relevant facts. Unless this were so, the set of beliefs would not be ideological. So, too, it would not be ideological if, in addition to its descriptive and prescriptive elements, it merely expressed the feelings of its propagators. To be ideological, it must be a set of beliefs to which a community or social group ordinarily resort in situations of a certain kind. They may, of course, resort to it (or to some part of it) to express or relieve their feelings, but it is their resorting to it that makes it ideological. An ideology, in this sense, is a possession or resource of a social group to be used on appropriate occasions.

At this point, the reader may feel that I am being arbitrary. Am I not insisting that a word should be used in a particular way rather than explaining how it is used? Did not Marx, who more than anyone introduced the word 'ideology' into social theory, speak of law and morality as ideological? Have not many sociologists followed his example? If anything is socially determined, and varies from society to society and from age to age, surely it is law and morality? When Pascal, though he was a mathematician and a physicist as well as a moralist, said that what is true on this side of the Pyrenees is error on the other, he was thinking, not of the theorems of Euclid or even of the system of Copernicus condemned by the Church, but of laws and moral rules. He differed from the sociologists of today in being willing to speak of rules of conduct as true or false (though in this instance he did so ironically), where they would rather speak of them as accepted or not accepted, as applying or not applying in a type of situation, as consistent with one another or not so, or as valid or invalid by reference to some standard distinct from them. Why, then, not call rules of conduct ideological? Why not follow the example of Marx and of others?

Because it makes for confusion of thought. Marx did not bother to distinguish rules from beliefs and arguments that support them. When he spoke of morality, he often meant indifferently both the rules and these supports of them, just as we all ordinarily do, unless we have some specific reason for not doing so. We often, when we speak of moral beliefs, have in mind both rules used to guide or influence conduct and propositions held to be true. For ordinary purposes there is no need to distinguish between them, but the social theorist ought to do so. Certainly, Marx would have done well to make the distinction, for if he had made it, he might have had clearer ideas than he did have about social relations. He tried to distinguish these relations from what he called the ideological superstructure, in which he included law and morality. But a social relation is essentially normative: the persons it relates have claims upon one another which they recognize or ought to recognize. The relation cannot be defined apart from the rules whose observance makes it the sort of relation it is.

I suggested earlier that it might be possible and useful to divide social relations into two kinds, calling the one kind 'primary' and the other 'secondary'. The division might perhaps be so made that secondary relations could plausibly be called ideological on the ground that they arise along with ideology. For example, wherever there are priests, there are distinctive relations among them and also between them and laymen. These relations can be defined only by reference to the beliefs and rites that constitute a religion; the priest is the teacher of these beliefs, the administrator of these rites. And religion is a form of ideology.

To take another example. There are specifically legal (as distinct from merely customary) rules only in communities or groups where the right to interpret certain rules and to enforce observance of them is confined to persons who acquire the right in prescribed ways. This, indeed, is what is ordinarily meant by calling them legal rules. Now, it is arguable that this right arises only in communities and groups where there are people who reflect about rules and come to hold certain beliefs about them and about their origins and uses; beliefs which they discuss sufficiently to be aware that they share them. In that case, they share something that can be called a legal theory, even though it is not set down in books and includes religious beliefs. This theory, to the extent that it serves to maintain feelings and dispositions which ensure that the interpreters of the law can carry out their functions, is ideological. It is arguable that wherever there are legal, as distinct from merely customary, rules there is an ideology of law.

The mark of moral rules is not that they are officially interpreted and enforced but that they are consciously set apart from other rules and are accorded a special status. There are beliefs connected with them—religious and other beliefs—which make people peculiarly reluctant to break them or to be suspected of having done so. Thus, except where there are select rules supported by beliefs which attribute a paramount status to them, there are (we may want to say) no specifically moral rules. These beliefs are shared by most people in the community and are known to be shared. So, we may argue, where there are properly moral rules, there are not only ideological beliefs that support them, there is some kind of theory of morals, rudimentary though it may be, which conspicuously sets some rules of conduct above others. It may be that Marx had vaguely in mind some such considerations as these when he relegated law and morality to the 'ideological superstructure'.

There is not to be found in the writings of Marx a clear account of law or morality, let alone ideology. He offers no precise definitions of them, and does not explain how they are related. But he does say of ideology that it is 'false consciousness'; it is an illusion more or less widely shared; it is persistent and pervasive. It consists of misconceptions about some important class of things or events shared by a community or group and expressed or implied by ways of thinking and speaking typical of them. Now, mere rules, no matter what their kind, are clearly not false consciousness. It is inconceivable that Marx, if he had been challenged, would have said that they were. He did not even believe that, wherever there are important social rules, there is also false consciousness. For example, he believed that in the communist society of the future there would be such rules but not that there would be misconceptions or illusions of the kind he called 'false consciousness'. In the communist society men will at last understand themselves and their environment as they really are. They will be able to do without the enforcement of rules by authority; they will not have law as we know it in bourgeois society. Nor will they be 'moral' in the way that men are in bourgeois society; they will not have the same attitudes to important social rules. Nevertheless, they will not be without rules, though they will be without false consciousness.

An ideology is always in large part descriptive. But it need not be false. That is to say, the word ideology, used in the sense I am now discussing, is often applied to sets of beliefs or to theories which are not false, or are so only to a small extent. They are accepted uncritically, or, if not always uncritically, then for other reasons besides their being thought to be true. No doubt, those who accept them believe that they are true, unless they merely pretend to accept them. Fantasy or fiction which is recognized to be so is not ideology, even though it expresses strong feelings and has important effects. Art is not ideology, though the purveyor of ideological beliefs is sometimes a great artist and often has something of the artist about him. Ideology inspires art but can find other than artistic expression, just as it can inspire both good art and bad and still be the same ideology. Yet art and ideology are closely related: much more closely than art and science, or art and common sense.

Marxists today do not speak of ideology as if it were always a form of false consciousness. They even use such expressions as 'the communist ideology' or 'the ideology of the proletariat': expressions which the older Marxists avoided. Perhaps when they call even Marxism an ideology they think of it as serving to hold a party or a class together and to guide their actions. When they think of it primarily as explaining the course of social change, they call it a theory. But here theory and ideology have the same contents, or else the ideology is thought of as the theory abridged. This theory or ideology is, they think, essentially true, though sometimes misapplied by those who accept it. Marxists are not perhaps readier than other men to admit their mistakes, but when they do admit them, the mistakes often turn out to have been big ones, and there is a lavish display of guilt and repentance. None the less, the ideology (though all too frequently misapplied) is held to be true in essentials. Yet the Marxists, who make this claim for it, also think of it as something different in kind from the ordinary empirical sciences, even the social sciences. When they call it 'scientific' (as they sometimes do) they use the word in a special sense. Their theory, as they conceive of it, is not like a theory in the empirical sciences; it is not a set of assumptions and principles that serve to relate to one another hypotheses that have been confirmed by experiment or some other kind of appeal to the facts, and to set up new hypotheses for confirmation. They claim for it, of course, that it is compatible with relevant hypotheses confirmed by these methods, but they also make, at least by implication, a larger claim than this. They think of it as an interpretation of history, of the course of social and cultural change, which brings out its 'significance' in a way that the theories of the mere sociologist and the explanations of the mere historian cannot do. It reveals the history of mankind as a progress in which men develop their capacities as they deepen their understanding of human nature and of the course of change in which their species is involved and so learn to control their environment and to achieve their aspirations as developed human beings.

The non-Marxist does not share the Marxist's estimate of his theory; he will see a great deal that is misconceived about it. Both the Marxism of Marx and the considerably different theories that now go by the name of Marxism-Leninism may seem to him as good examples as any of false consciousness. And yet he may concede that the appeal of these theories lies, not so much in those of their doctrines that can be shown to be self-contradictory, confused or contrary to the facts, as in a conception of man which may be unverifiable but is nevertheless intelligible. It is the idea of man as a being who develops capacities peculiar to his kind and so becomes self-aware and rational, through activities whereby he brings into existence a social world and an order of ideas in terms of which he defines himself and his environment; a being involved in a course of change in which he and his social world are continually transformed and he is inhibited in ways that eventually deepen his self-knowledge and increase his control over his environment; a being who will learn at last to take the measure of his own needs and aspirations and to act rationally to satisfy them. This idea of man as a self-transforming and progressive being is neither self-contradictory nor unintelligible. Though historians and social theorists today accept some parts of it they do not, unless they are Marxists, accept it as a whole. It is not, taken as a whole, the body of assumptions on which their explanations rest. Nor is it an idea of man that all men share. It is not an hypothesis, or rather a set of hypotheses, that the sociologist or the historian can confirm or show to be false. Neither is it a programme of action or a moral code or a pack of value judgements dressed up to look like a description. Though people who accept this idea may be disposed also to accept certain values, to formulate the idea is not to define the values.

Nor is the idea a misconception. To accept it is not to misunderstand either men's motives, feelings and intentions or their institutions and ideas. Still less is it to assert the existence of beings or the occurrence of events outside the range of everyday experience or unknown to the empirical sciences. It is not a form of false consciousness, and it is not empty.

No doubt, from this idea *alone*, nothing follows. I have put it summarily and, I dare say, inadequately; but, even if it were put more fully, in a way that did better justice to it, nothing would follow from it alone. It is, so I believe, an idea that can be extracted from Marx's writings, though he did not himself formulate it clearly. But anyone can accept it without being bound in logic to accept Marx's views about how existence is related to 'consciousness', or his account of the capitalist economy or of the bourgeois state or of classes and the conflicts between them—or any other doctrine of his that can be confirmed or disproved empirically. (Not that I wish to disparage any of these doctrines. Though they are all to some extent obscure, and none is acceptable as a whole, they contain ideas and hints of ideas of great value to the social scientist or the historian. Marx's writings abound in good ideas.)

Whoever accepts the idea of man that I have tried to summarize must also accept other ideas if he is to be able to construct hypotheses that can be tested by an appeal to the facts or to draw practical conclusions. These other ideas he need not take from Marx. But wherever he takes them, he will combine them with his conception: a conception which, as we have seen, is by no means a simple one. This conception of man will not preclude him from accepting the conclusions that the social scientist reaches by empirical methods, though it may move him to reformulate some of them so that they are more in keeping with his conception. And it will, of course, often move him to draw from the facts practical conclusions which he otherwise would not draw.

The Marxist, to deserve the name, must take much more from Marx than this idea of man. If he took only this idea, he would not be reckoned a Marxist. Indeed, it is an idea that Marx never put clearly, and that many Marxists have taken over without fully understanding it, despite the many echoes of it in their thinking. If they were asked what was specifically Marxist about their beliefs, they would point probably, not to this idea, but to more familiar and more obscure doctrines, some of them with a good deal of 'false consciousness' about them—doctrines that seem less obscure only because they are more familiar, having long been encapsulated in neat phrases. But my present business is not to assess the claims for Marxism made by Marxists. I have merely used Marxism to help me reach this conclusion: that an ideology with nothing of 'false consciousness' about it is in principle possible. An ideology of this kind would not consist just of science and history with a prescriptive element added to them. It would contain also an idea of man, an interpretation of his activities, compatible with but not presupposed by the findings of the psychologist and the sociologist. Yet this idea would be a product of reflection, a fruit of experience. It would be a belief or set of beliefs about man and not just a feeling or attitude or disposition expressed in words.

Though a conception of this kind is not in itself an illusion, it can form part of an ideology having a large dose of illusion to it. There is perhaps to be found in every philosophy or dogmatic religion which has had a deep influence on believers some such idea of man: an idea which is neither an illusion nor a verifiable hypothesis, nor yet an assumption on which common sense or scientific accounts of human behaviour rest.

Marx included in 'false consciousness' all forms of religious beliefs, but there are other social theorists who, though they too are without religion, do not accept Marx's account of it, or accept it only in part. They concede that there are religious beliefs that the empirical studies, scientific and historical, can neither confirm nor disprove, and that these beliefs are none the less intelligible. They are not beliefs about man; they are not ideas of the kind that I have been discussing. Marx might call them fantasies, but these other social theorists would hesitate to do so, and not just from a desire to speak respectfully of harmless or even useful beliefs which they do not share. Illusions and fantasies, as we commonly speak of them, concern things and events within the range of ordinary experience, whereas these beliefs do not. People who accept beliefs of this kind also accept some idea or other of man. The beliefs and the idea are, in their minds, intimately connected. Some of the beliefs are, indeed, about God or the gods in relation to man. But there can be extracted from them an idea of man which could be defined without reference to other than human beings.

Religion as ideology

It was not really until the eighteenth century that political theorists and philosophers in the West began seriously to enquire how it comes about that men have religious beliefs. Until then, they had confined themselves to examining the doctrines of the theologians, especially their proofs of the existence of God, accepting some and amending or rejecting others. They had sometimes expressed doubts about traditional accounts of the origins of particular religions, but had had little to say about the origins of religion in general or its place in the life of man, or about the different kinds of religion. Ordinarily, they had approved of religion as a support of morals, and had deplored religious fanaticism; for example, Machiavelli, who thought religion a good thing. The founders of religions are, he thought, even more to be admired than founders of states as benefactors of mankind. Though he took care not to deny that Christianity is of divine origin, he clearly thought of the founders of other religions as inspired predominantly by political motives. Hobbes was less inclined to praise the founders of religion, though he said nothing against them. There are, he said, men who claim that God has spoken to them and who pass on his message to other men; there are prophets, false and true. It is for the ruler to decide who the true prophets are, since diversity of religious beliefs is a danger to domestic peace. Most political theorists, even champions of toleration such as Locke, condemned atheism.

In the eighteenth century there was, as never before, speculation about the worldly origins of religious beliefs and myths. They are, it was said, products of curiosity, ignorance and fear. It is because man is capable of putting questions and of discovering or inventing answers to them that he has beliefs as distinct from mere habits and expectations. In the 'childhood' of the race, man puts childlike questions and gives childlike answers. He does not understand how he differs from the other animals, and has not learned to distinguish the inanimate from the animate. He attributes to other animals and to lifeless things feelings and intentions similar to his own. He is a prey to many fears, which he seeks to allay by propitiating spirits that he believes to be hostile to him. As knowledge increases, man learns to put more sophisticated questions and to give more sophisticated answers. Religion, at least for the educated, sheds its grosser superstitions and becomes more coherent, or it loses its hold altogether. This explanation of religion takes notice chiefly of its psychological and cognitive origins.

Other thinkers, notably Montesquieu, were more concerned with its social functions and the social conditions that favour or impede the growth of particular religions. Islam, said Montesquieu, spread rapidly among the Arabs and other peoples with institutions and mores similar to theirs but in Europe its progress was arrested because it was unsuited to established customs and manners. The philosophers of the Enlightenment attacked

4

the Church rather than religion. They accused the priests of having a vested interest in maintaining superstition and exploiting credulity. But few of them believed that it was either possible or desirable to loosen the hold of religion on the uneducated. What they wanted, above all, was freedom of thought for themselves and for the educated classes for whom they wrote. They wanted, not to abolish religion, but to prevent its abuse by churchmen. These ways of thinking about religion have persisted into the nineteenth and twentieth centuries, among both unbelievers and believers. Anti-clericalism has never been confined to persons who are without faith.

There was also another conception of religion which has had a profound influence on modern ways of thinking about the place of both religion and philosophy in the life of man. It inspired the most original and exciting of Hegel's works, *The Phenomenology of Spirit*, but the most admirable and moving expression of it goes back to the seventeenth century, to the *Pensées* of Pascal, the notes for a book that was never completed. (This work was not published until long after Pascal's death, and the whole of what survives of it not until the nineteenth century.) Man needs religion to give him a sense of place in the world, a sense of his own identity, an idea of himself that satisfies him; for, without it, he, who differs from other animals in being self-conscious, is intolerable to, and seeks to escape from, himself. Religion satisfies an essential need of a creature that is an object of thought to itself, and therefore aware of itself as a finite being in an infinite world. If man can see no purpose and no reason in the world other than his own, then, since he knows that he is ephemeral, inconstant and frail, he feels himself to be a lost being, a finite mind in a mindless universe, a feeble light in a dark wilderness. Pascal, himself a scientist and a mathematician, was terrified by the scientist's image of a limitless mechanical world in which all events happen necessarily in accordance with immutable laws. He saw rooted in man's capacity to reason—the capacity that gives birth to science—a need that science cannot satisfy. He himself believed that only the Christian religion in its Catholic form can satisfy this need. But the *Pensées*, his greatest work, is less impressive perhaps as an argument for Christianity than as an explanation of the need for religion. One of the implications of the argument is that this need is never more intensely felt than by men who understand what science is and are impressed by its achievements.

There are traces of this idea of religion in the writings of Rousseau. Religion does not only provide men with additional motives for behaving well, or bring them closer together in community of faith, or console them when they suffer; it also provides them with a conception of man's place in the world which makes life worth living. This conception, so Rousseau believed, was of a kind that the sciences, whose progress he did not deny, could not provide. He was not as much an enemy of the sciences as he sometimes pretended to be; he admitted that they destroy harmful prejudices and superstitions. Rousseau spoke of religion in such a way as to suggest that man's need of it goes deeper than his need of science. It is a need that does not grow weaker with the progress of the sciences, though that progress may make us less aware of it and less able to satisfy it. Hence the unhappiness of men whose pride in reason puts faith out of their reach.

Kant held that there are three beliefs necessary to man if he is to be moral and happy: he must believe in God, in the freedom of the will, and in immortality. These are not beliefs that can be proved to be true either empirically or by *a priori* reasoning. Man, in so far as he acts in specifically human ways, is essentially a moral being, and he cannot act morally unless he can choose freely how he shall act. The phenomenal world (which includes the phenomenal self), the world as it necessarily appears to man, is a world in which everything is causally determined. And yet, according to Kant, if man is to be able to act morally, he must have freedom of the will in a sense of freedom which entails that his decisions are not causally determined. The man who acts morally may not, often does not, achieve happiness in this world; and yet justice requires that he shall achieve it, which he can do only in a life after death. Kant was less concerned that men should believe they had an interest in behaving well than that justice should be done. God, in his eyes, was something more than a dispenser of rewards and punishments who sees all and leaves nothing unrewarded or unpunished. Without these beliefs, there is no sense and dignity to the life of man.

We have seen that, for Hegel, the course of human history is the self-revelation of Spirit at the levels of self-consciousness and reason. How men see themselves and the world is how Spirit sees itself. Hence the great interest that Hegel took in the history of religion and philosophy. Religion, as he saw it, expresses figuratively what philosophy seeks to make explicit. There is progress in both religion and philosophy. Spirit, at certain stages of its dialectical movement towards self-knowledge, sees the world, which is merely a projection of itself, as something alien to it. Hegel spoke of it, therefore, as estranged or alienated from itself. But Spirit aspires to a full self-knowledge, a full self-possession. This estrangement from itself is a painful experience, an experience to be lived through and passed beyond. It is a condition of itself that Spirit must overcome. This condition, the need to overcome it, and the assurance that it will be overcome, all find symbolic expression in religion; or, rather, in a type of religion in which men (the finite rational beings in whose activities and ideas Spirit is manifest) see themselves estranged from a God whose creatures they are and without whom they are nothing, aspiring to union with him and destined to be united.

Marx's idea of religion as a fantasy of alienated man, though it owes a great deal to Hegel, is different in two important respects. Marx rejects completely the notion of Spirit. It is man alone that is alienated, and not anything manifest in him, and when man overcomes this alienation, there is no place for religion. Though society is a product of human activities, and also consists of them, men have to learn to recognize it for what it is, and the learning is slow and painful. They must first see society as something alien to them, that inhibits and oppresses them, before they can learn to control it. Their image of the natural world is also, to begin with, an image of something alien and hostile. It is only as they come to understand their environment, natural and social, and learn to adapt it to their purposes, that they cease to look upon it as alien and hostile, that they come gradually to see it as the environment in which they develop their specifically human capacities. Living and working together to satisfy their natural appetites, they produce the social world and the ideas they use; they generate, over and above the appetites they are born with or acquire as their bodies mature, needs and aspirations peculiar to social beings, arising out of and yet also thwarted by their own social activities until such time as they come to understand the needs and aspirations and the activities. For the understanding of both necessarily grows together. Since man is essentially a social being, in the sense that the capacities peculiar to his species are developed in him by social intercourse, his specifically human needs and aspirations have no meaning apart from the social world, the system of his social activities.

In religion man sees himself as subject to higher beings, whom he nevertheless sees in his own image. Religion expresses his sense that he is not yet his own master, that he has not yet learned to adapt his environment to his needs, that he is the victim of circumstances as yet beyond his control, and it expresses also his aspiration to be his own master. Religion is a form of false consciousness, it is ideology; it is not an effect of mere ignorance. It does not consist of explanations that the ignorant make do with for want of something better; it does much more than reinforce morality by promising rewards and threatening punishments in an after-life; it consists of more than attempts to propitiate malevolent spirits and to invoke the help of benevolent ones. It reflects the human condition at a stage in the historical process when man is still incapable of understanding that condition. If he understood it, he would not need to give religious expression to it. He cannot understand it except in the process of overcoming it, for to understand it is to understand how it comes about that he is a victim of his own lack of understanding. It is to get rid of the illusions in which the condition is rooted and which it cannot survive.

Religion, thus conceived, is a fantasy that compensates men for their failure to be what they aspire to be. They are not, in the social world, though it consists only of their activities, their own masters; they are the victims of circumstances of their own making but outside their control, and are degraded in their own eyes. Their abasement of themselves before God, a creature of their own imagination, expresses this degradation; their aspiration to union with God in an after-life expresses their sense of what they might be and are not. They seek, in imagination, in the fantasy of a life after death, the satisfaction denied to them in this life. They seek but do not find, for they can get real satisfaction only by learning to control society and to achieve their purposes in it. It is a condition of their getting it that they should get rid of religion, that they should rise above 'false consciousness', above the illusions that are marks of human impotence and immaturity. This men can do, not by the mere pursuit of knowledge for its own sake, but in the process of transforming society, first without aiming to do so, in the pursuit of other goals, and later deliberately. In transforming society they transform themselves. They learn to stand on their own feet; they get out from under the shadow of the gods they have themselves fashioned.

If this is what religion is, then clearly there is much more to it than class ideology. Yet it has a good deal in common with class ideology, as Marxists understand it. This, no doubt, explains why Marxists find it so easy to speak at times as if all ideology were class ideology, though they also call religion a form of ideology. Just as religion expresses man's attitude to his own species in the form of a system of beliefs about the world as a whole, so a class ideology expresses the attitude of a class to itself in the form of a system of beliefs about society, about the social world. Bourgeois ideology is more than just a set of beliefs that promote the interests of a class by justifying its claims; it is also an image of society that expresses the bourgeois attitude to man. Since man is a social being, his conception of himself is revealed in his conception of the society in which he has his being. Bourgeois ideology takes the form of social theory rather than religion. But religion often has the rudiments of a social theory wrapped up in it: even the religion of a primitive community in which there are neither social classes nor deliberate attempts to explain society.

Marx spoke of religion as a fantasy of alienated man. He did not except from this general verdict the religions of primitive peoples, even though what he took to be a major cause of alienation (the extensive division of labour) is not found among such peoples. His ideas about alienation and religion do not fit nicely together into a consistent whole. Nevertheless, the religions which come closest to being, or appearing to be, fantasies of alienated man flourish in societies which, economically, are not primitive. Alienation, if not confined to such societies, takes in them a sharper form. Or, at least, it can be argued that it does. But economically developed societies are also class societies. If this line of reasoning is accepted, then it would seem to follow that religion is most likely to be a fantasy of alienated man where there are classes and class ideologies.

We have considered five different but not unrelated conceptions of religion as ideology, as a system of beliefs that communities or other social groups resort to regardless of their truth, because they satisfy a need. 1. Religion is an effect of ignorance and curiosity, and consists of fantasies that give men the illusion that they have knowledge where they in fact lack it; it is a substitute for knowledge to which they resort while they are as yet unable to answer certain questions that move them deeply, or else cannot see that the questions are unanswerable or unintelligible. 2. Religion serves to allay fears and to give an outlet to passions to which men are liable because of their ignorance and their inability to control the forces of nature. 3. It serves to hold communities and groups together by giving a public and sacred character to certain actions and occasions; as, for example, marriages or burials, or settlements of disputes. 4. It serves to reinforce men's motives for observing social rules by the threat of punishments or the promise of rewards at the hands of some being or beings more powerful than man. 5. It provides man with a conception of himself and of his place in the world that satisfies him, or it expresses feelings which he has about himself and his condition, often without being aware that he has them.

5/Class Ideology and Class-Consciousness

Social groups: interests and ideologies

We have seen that social groups are defined in terms of the social activities typical of their members, and that all social activities involve the use of ideas. If, then, we want to enquire how the activities of a group affect its ideas, or are affected by them, the ideas we have in mind are presumably not those involved in the activities, but other ideas. These ideas can include beliefs about the activities or can express attitudes towards them. Social groups are also defined in terms of social relations, but then social relations are themselves defined in terms of the social activities typical of the persons they relate. The ideology of a group consists, not of the 'ideas' (using this word broadly to refer to any kind of thinking) forming part of the activities typical of it, but of other ideas. If we call the first ideas 'primary', we may call the others 'secondary'. The ideology of a group consists only of secondary ideas, but this, of course, does not imply that all such ideas are ideological.

Not all societies are divided into classes. Societies that are classless also have secondary ideas, some of which are ideological. Ideology is not necessarily class ideology, nor consciousness necessarily class consciousness. Not, that is to say, unless the word 'class' is used so broadly that any social group is a class. As a matter of fact, the word never is used in so broad a sense, not even by the Marxists when they speak (as at times they do) as if all ideology were class ideology. The word 'class', though used in more than one sense, is always used to refer only to some kinds of groups.

Class relations and roles, like all others, involve the use of ideas. If Peter is a master and James his slave, Peter's master-like behaviour towards James involves the use of ideas, and so does James's servile behaviour towards him. The ideas they use in social intercourse between them, in sustaining their roles, are in many respects the same. Peter and James both speak of Peter as the master, and when they speak to one another, the senses in which they use the word are much the same. But Peter is not the only master, nor James the only slave; they belong to a society in which there are many masters and many slaves. The maintenance of slavery as an institution depends largely on social intercourse between masters. The masters when they talk to one another about their slaves, or when they discuss the institution of slavery and what they must do to maintain it, will use ideas they do not use in their dealings with their slaves. They may, of course, convey these ideas by using words which they also use in speaking to their slaves; they may merely use them in different senses. These ideas that the masters use among themselves are secondary. They are ideas typical of the masters as a class. To the extent that they serve to maintain the institution of slavery (for example, by justifying it), they are ideological; and they are a class ideology in so far as they are typical of a class. And the same can be said of the ideas typical of slaves which serve to maintain slavery. As we shall see later, the term 'class ideology' is used to cover more ideas than these. For example, it is used to cover the 'revolutionary' ideas of a class, and such ideas, clearly, do not serve to maintain the institutions or social relations which give to that class its class character. Still, whatever else the ideology of a class may consist of, it consists at least of beliefs and attitudes that help to ensure that people who belong to the class sustain their class roles.

Now, it is not clear why class ideology, thus conceived, need have anything of illusion or false consciousness about it. For example, the beliefs of masters about slavery might differ considerably from the beliefs of slaves, and yet the two sets of beliefs both be true. Masters and slaves might have some beliefs about slavery in common, and others peculiar to their class, and yet all the beliefs be true. Or, if some were false, they might be the beliefs held in common and not ones confined to a class.

Nobody denies that there are plenty of false beliefs typical of this or that social group. Just as nobody denies that the beliefs of one group are often inconsistent with those of another. The difficulty, as we shall see later, is not in understanding how there can be false consciousness or how the beliefs of different groups can be inconsistent with one another: the difficulty rather is to understand why paramount importance among group ideologies should be ascribed to class ideologies, or why it should be held that they are more likely than others to be widely divergent, or why some classes should be thought more liable than others to false consciousness.

If we take any asymmetrical social relation, we can always distinguish two categories of persons according to how they stand in that relation. Masters are not related to slaves as slaves are to masters, and therefore we can distinguish masters from slaves. Similarly, husbands are not related to wives as wives are to husbands; their social roles differ. But, whereas the institution of slavery generates two classes, the institution of marriage does not. Let us say that it generates two social categories. If we take either of these two relations, slavery and marriage, we can, in principle, distinguish three uses of ideas connected with it. First, we have the primary ideas, the ones used in the actual performance of the social roles that constitute the relation. I have supposed that these ideas are often much the same for both classes or categories. Second, we have ideas about the relation shared by the two classes or categories or peculiar to one of them. The ideas that are not shared could diverge widely without being inconsistent with one another, for they could be just complementary. Those of them used descriptively could all be true, and those used to make value judgements or to express feelings could be mutually compatible. The shared ideas, like the ones not shared, could be either true or false, compatible or incompatible, but there is no obvious reason why they should be less often false or incompatible than the ideas peculiar to one class or category.

Last, we have a more 'reflective' use of ideas to construct explanations that 'place' the relation or institution in a larger context, for example, in the life of the community or even in the divine scheme of things. These explanations, too, may be rudimentary and gain currency among the illiterate and so scarcely deserve to be called theories, or they may be elaborate and deliberately put together by literate and sophisticated persons. Yet I shall venture to call them theories even when they are rudimentary, for they are not just sets of beliefs but attempts to explain how some part of life fits into a larger context. There are, of course, more of these explanations produced by literate than by illiterate persons, but they are not confined to the literate or invented only by them. There are the rudiments of theory even in the most primitive communities; there are to be found, even in them, systems of explanatory beliefs recognized as such by the persons who hold them and not only by the sociologists who study them.

If we take the first sort of ideas (those used in actually carrying out social roles, in sustaining social relations) there would appear to be little that is illusory about them. Merely to use them is not to have what can properly be called false consciousness. They are used for the most part to make and to meet claims, to give orders or to make requests that the givers and makers feel they are entitled to give and to make. No doubt, they would be incapable of making and meeting claims if they were incapable of understanding any description of the social relations in which they stand, of deciding whether they were true or false. But they need not themselves make such descriptions in order to play their parts in sustaining the relations. Indeed, the making and meeting of claims does not even involve, necessarily, making value judgements; it involves only the capacity to make them should the need arise. For example, a man makes a request of a woman which he would not make if she were not his wife. If she complies, he says no more. If she demurs, he reminds her that she is his wife. If that is not enough, he reminds her of her duties as a wife. If even that is not enough, he perhaps goes so far, wisely or unwisely, as to lecture her about marriage. He resorts to ideas of our second and third kinds in support of claims which he actually makes by using ideas of the first kind.

It is his interest as a husband that his claims should be met. But in supporting these claims against his wife, when he finds her reluctant to meet them, he is perhaps ill advised to use ideas (if there are any) peculiar to husbands. He would perhaps do better to use ideas shared by husbands and wives, or even (if he could make them serve his turn) ideas more widely accepted among wives than among husbands. All these ideas, equally, would be ideological. The husband might or might not have examined them critically and satisfied himself that they were true or valid, but he would be using them to support the claims he was making as a husband. That would be enough to make them ideological. But would it be enough to make them husbands' ideology as distinct from wives' ideology? Let me leave that question unanswered for the moment. For husbands are merely a social category and not a class, and it may be that a social category does not have a group ideology in the sense that a social class has. Its members, we have seen, have ideological beliefs which they use to support the claims they make, and also of course to resist claims made upon them. Yet these beliefs may not constitute a group ideology distinct from those of other groups.

It is often said of ideological beliefs that they promote the interests of the persons who hold them. So, before we enquire what a group ideology is, we should ask first what it is for a group to have interests. Sometimes, when we speak of the interests of a group, we mean the aims typical of its members, aims that most of them have and that are rare outside the group. At other times, we mean the conditions that favour the achievement of these typical aims. Often, the term 'group interests' is used to cover both these things. Though these are not its only uses, they are perhaps the most frequent. Marxists also speak of the 'objective interests' of a class, but this is a difficult notion to which I shall return later.

If we take the interests of a group to mean the typical aims of its members, then the persons who have these aims know their own interests. To say that they do is only to say that they know what they want. Yet they may not know that most persons in the group have these aims. Indeed, the group that they belong to may mean very little to them; they may scarcely be aware that they belong to it. It may be important only to the sociologist. But, even if they are aware that they belong to it, they may not know which of their aims are typical of the group. For example, a man may know that he is a peasant and yet not know which of his aims are shared by most peasants but by few people who are not peasants. Or he may know that these aims of his are widely shared in the group he belongs to and yet not know what conditions favour their achievement.

Ideological beliefs not only serve to maintain social relations (or to subvert them, though we have not yet considered their subversive effects), they also promote group interests. They do so, for example, by making the members of the group more aware than they otherwise would be that they share certain aims and that certain conditions favour their achievement. But we ought not, as social theorists sometimes do (for they seldom do it consistently), speak of these ideological beliefs as if they were determined by the group's interests. If we say that they 'reflect' their interests, intending to assert only a correlation between them and what they reflect, this makes good enough sense: though, as we shall see later, it needs to be qualified, since ideological beliefs can sometimes be out of keeping with the interests of the persons whose beliefs they are. Beliefs and interests continually affect one another. For example, the aims typical of wives who belong to the same community or class are affected by their beliefs about marriage, by what I have called their secondary ideas, and in their turn affect these beliefs. The pursuit of these aims can alter the character of marriage, and yet not be successful. So we have here three things—an institution or social relation, a set of ideological beliefs, and the interests of persons involved in the relation—which continually affect one another but are not therefore necessarily compatible. Either the relation or the beliefs can be such that they impede the pursuit of the interests.

Let us now get back to social classes, and to their interests and ideologies. Classes have been distinguished from one another in several different ways. Marx distinguished them according to the type of property people owned or did not own; others have distinguished them in terms of wealth or status or power or influence. Though these things are closely connected—though, for example, owners of certain types of property tend to be wealthy, and the wealthy tend to have high status and considerable power—the lines of division between classes distinguished in these different ways do not always coincide. But we need not, for our purpose, consider how the criteria used to define classes differ and what 'social map' we get by using one set of criteria rather than another. More important, from our point of view, is to distinguish between two kinds of social groups, and to notice that a social class can be a group of either kind. Let us call groups of the first kind 'passive', and groups of the second kind 'active'.

A social group (or category) consists of the persons who stand in the social relations or have the interests or beliefs that define the group.* If they do not know that they share these interests or beliefs, or do not act together to promote them, they are a passive group. Thus, husbands are ordinarily a passive group, and

*I use the term 'social group' to refer to any set of persons having interests, purposes, activities, beliefs, sentiments, attitudes, rights or obligations that distinguish them from others. The term, I know, is often used more narrowly to refer to persons congregated together, or acting together for a common purpose, or moved to action by similar purposes or motives, but I need to use the term more broadly than that. 'Social class' will not do for my purpose, and I prefer to speak of groups rather than categories.

so too are wives, and so are married persons. Husbands and wives are, taken individually, often very active indeed, putting a great deal of energy into being husbands or into being wives. But as groups they are ordinarily passive. Some classes are or have been passive groups. Marx, in the *Eighteenth Brumaire*, suggested that the French peasants were so at the time that Louis Bonaparte became president of the French Republic; he did not call them a passive group but said that they lacked 'class consciousness'.

Sometimes, members of two or more social groups, especially when they are passive, have little to do with one another. For example, peasants often have little to do with urban workers while both groups are passive, though later, when they become active, they have more to do with one another, as they compete for favours from the government or act together to promote interests common to them. Even then, of course, for most workers and peasants, these dealings are vicarious; it is their leaders who compete or co-operate on their behalf. But members of two social groups can be very much involved with one another in carrying on the social roles peculiar to them, even though both groups are passive or one is so. For example, husbands and wives. Or masters and slaves, for though masters are usually active groups, slaves are not. Masters act together, as masters, in a way that husbands do not. For though men who are husbands have many dealings with one another they have them not as husbands so much as in other capacities. Slaves of the same master are, of course, in close touch with one another just as, in countries that practise polygamy, wives of the same husband are. These slaves or wives may act together to further their interests against their master or husband. To that extent they are an active group. But their situation is very different from one in which a considerable proportion of a large social category acts together for this purpose.

The frequent intercourse, at work and at leisure, between members of the same group, an intercourse that sharpens their

awareness that they share certain aims and beliefs, is not confined to social classes. It is often greater among men who do the
same kind of work, among lawyers or butchers or farmers. These
occupational groups tend to be very active indeed, and sometimes compete fiercely with one another. But there is an important difference between social classes and occupational groups.
When a class becomes an active group it often does so to defend
its interests against another class closely bound up with it. For
example, the masters of slaves act together to protect their
interests against the slaves. No doubt, they also act together to
protect their interests against other groups. Slave owners in the
United States had to defend their class interests against groups
other than slaves. But an institution such as slavery binds the
classes involved in it close to one another. Not so close, no doubt,
as marriage, but still very close. So, too, capitalists and workers,
or feudal landowners and serfs, are in this same way involved
with one another. Not all classes are involved in this way with
some other class. Yeoman farmers, for example, are not. But
many classes are. Nor, of course, are classes the only groups thus
involved. Officers in the armed forces are not a social class, nor
are the men under them, though in many countries officers do
ordinarily belong to a different class from other ranks. It often
happens that in large organizations with a well-defined hierarchy, higher and lower ranks are recruited from different
classes; and also, in countries claiming to be classless but
with many large organizations in them, that higher and
lower ranks soon acquire some of the characteristics of separate
classes.

Classes differ from other social groups in two conspicuous
ways: they are more *comprehensive* in the sense that their members
take part together in a larger range of activities and are related
to one another more variously than members of most other
groups; and they are more *exclusive* in the sense that movement
from class to class is unusually irksome and disturbing. People
ordinarily marry within the class they belong to, engage in most

of their leisure activities with other members of it, enter occupations or ranks in a hierarchy largely confined to it; and they find it difficult and even painful to move out of the class to which their parents belong. Notoriously, classes differ considerably in both comprehensiveness and exclusiveness. Though many social theorists have pointed to these two characteristics of classes, most of them have not used them as defining characteristics. They have preferred to use other criteria to distinguish between classes, presumably because it is impossible to decide just how comprehensive and exclusive a social group must be to count as a class. But it is worth noticing that a sparsely populated country with many classes could have classes more comprehensive and exclusive than a thickly populated country with only a few. This could be so even if differences of wealth and power and education were greater in the second country than the first. The comprehensiveness of a class varies, not with the proportion of the population that it includes or with the range of differences in wealth or power inside it, but with the extent of the social intercourse confined to its members.

Class ideology

Many social groups have common interests and ideological beliefs. They may not have theories, or not more than the rudiments of theory, but they have ideological beliefs either confined to them or shared by them with others. And the shared beliefs may serve as much as the unshared to promote their interests. In what ways, then, and under what circumstances, are classes and their interests and ideological beliefs especially important?

Classes are sometimes distinguished from castes and from estates, but for our purpose it is better to treat castes and estates as species of class. In societies where there are castes or estates, there is little or no movement of individuals from one caste or estate into another. Ideological beliefs in such societies serve to maintain the established order and are rarely subversive, though there are sometimes small groups outside the system of castes or estates or else cutting across them whose ideologies are subversive. The poorer and more illiterate castes or estates have only the rudiments of theory, for it is among the wealthier, the more powerful and the more literate that theories (that is to say, more or less definite and comprehensive accounts of society or of the world) take hold. These theories, though no doubt they affect the beliefs of the humbler groups, are the possessions of the more exalted, of those who govern and take it upon themselves to maintain the established order. There are, in these caste or feudal societies, classes and class interests and also beliefs that serve to further these interests. Yet the interests and beliefs are not recognized for what they are. There is virtually no speculation about them, even though there are theories about the social order which explain the different roles of the estates or castes inside it.

Where classes are highly exclusive, society tends to change slowly—so slowly that people are not aware that it changes. Where classes are less exclusive, society tends to change more quickly, and people are aware that it does change. Social change, social mobility and awareness of social change tend to reinforce one another. As social mobility increases, the idea gradually takes hold that it is for every man to make his own place in society. People come increasingly to believe that institutions do, or ought to, help men to get what they want. Egalitarian and liberal doctrines gain in popularity, and the conviction grows that the established order favours some classes unduly compared with others. People become more sharply aware that the interests and the beliefs of classes differ, and are often incompatible. It is then that there arise acute class conflicts. They arise largely because people come to accept principles whose realization requires that classes should disappear.

Interests and beliefs can differ greatly without producing conflict or disharmony. The typical aims of two social groups may differ, and yet neither group stand in the way of the other. Or, if they do stand in each other's way, neither group may know that it does. On the other hand, the typical aims of two groups may be closely similar and yet conditions be such that the more one group achieves its aims, the less the other can achieve its. If the groups become aware that this is so, there can arise bitter conflicts between them. For example, conflicts of interest between greater and lesser nobles can be (and have been) more bitter than conflicts between nobles and peasants.

So, too, with ideological beliefs, we must not confuse difference with incompatibility. If we take into account only personal aims (what men want for themselves and their dependents), we may find that two groups have aims that are very similar. In that case, it is likely that those of their beliefs that 'support' these aims (that serve to define and justify them) will also be similar. But if we take the conditions that favour the achievement of these aims, we may find that they differ considerably for the two groups. In that case, the beliefs that 'support' conditions favourable to one group will differ from the beliefs 'supporting' conditions favourable to the other. The two groups will then share some beliefs but not others. Yet there may be no conflicts between them, for these conditions, though different, may be compatible with one another. Only if they are incompatible, or are thought to be so by one or both of the groups, is there likely to be conflict.

It is often said that in some western countries most people (or at least most people seriously interested in politics) are liberals, whether they belong to the Right or the Left. If they are so, it is presumably because they have broadly similar beliefs about the range of allowable personal aims and about the opportunities and rights people must have to be able to pursue these aims effectively. Yet there are sharp and even bitter conflicts between these liberals, presumably because they differ about the conditions, social and economic, for providing these opportunities. They may come much closer than people did two or three centuries ago to having similar social and political philosophies, and yet conflicts between them may be just as sharp or even sharper.

I suggest that awareness of classes and of divergencies of interest and belief between them heightens as classes grow less exclusive and their interests and beliefs grow more alike, though not necessarily more compatible. Marxists, I dare say, would call this suggestion absurd, and it is nowhere to be found in the works of the master. Yet Marx did sometimes say things in keeping with it; as, for example, when he used the word 'class' in a narrower sense than he ordinarily used it. For he sometimes spoke of classes as if they were peculiar to capitalist societies, contrasting them with the 'estates' of feudal Europe. He sometimes spoke of the 'bourgeois' as if they were the first class, properly so called, to arise as the feudal society of the Middle Ages disintegrated and a new type of social and political order emerged. The bourgeois were, to begin with, a 'revolutionary' class; in promoting their class interests, they put forward claims on behalf of all men; they propounded a liberal and egalitarian creed teaching that all men, merely by virtue of being human, have certain rights which it is the business of the state to protect. This, so Marx tells us, is the theory of it. But practice does not correspond to theory because the workers, who have no property (or, rather, whose sole property is the labour-power they must sell to keep themselves alive) cannot exercise the rights claimed for all men, and because the wealthy either control the state or are so placed in relation to it that it protects their rights and interests to the detriment of the propertyless. The propertyless will eventually rise against the social and political order that oppresses them; and Marx, sometimes at least, speaks of this rising as if its aim were to get for the oppressed the freedom (the rights and opportunities) due to all men though in practice denied to most of them. There are occasions (for example, in *The Eighteenth Brumaire of Louis Bonaparte*), when Marx comes close to ascribing much the same principles to bourgeois and proletarians, and to suggesting that the bourgeois, unlike the proletarians, cannot afford to be true to them though they use them to promote their class interests.

Marx conceived of the communist society, which he thought would eventually result from a successful revolution made by the propertyless, as a social order in which there would be no state, and therefore presumably no law and no legal rights as we know them today. Just what he had in mind when he spoke of the 'stateless' society of the future is a matter of controversy. Yet the opportunities which he thought everyone would have in the communist society are (I suggest) not unlike those claimed by 'bourgeois' liberals for all men.* But my purpose, at the moment, is not to prove that Marx was a liberal, for these brief comments on some things he said or implied are not enough to do that. Though I believe that I have not misinterpreted these particular things, I shall not defend my interpretation of them. I allude to them only to illustrate a thesis which may be true, even if I have misinterpreted them: that conflicts of interest and ideology between classes can grow more acute as classes become less exclusive and the aims and beliefs of their members grow more alike. I do not say that this must be so always, I merely suggest that it has been so in the West in the last few centuries, and again more recently in non-western countries influenced by the West.

As classes have grown less exclusive (or, as some may prefer to put it, as estates or castes have made way for classes), class ideologies have become less theological and more social and political. They have also, in general, become more theoretical, that is, more often deliberately produced by professional thinkers or more influenced by such productions. In becoming more theoretical they have not necessarily gained in coherence. They owe more than they used to do to books and are more affected by controversies between intellectuals. They are no doubt more voluminous and more sophisticated; they take account of many

---

*Liberals often and readily admit that, even in the West, most people lack these opportunities: an admission for which the Marxists rarely give them credit.

more things and make important distinctions that used not to be made. But they are not therefore more coherent. In a primitive society most people may share the same beliefs and these beliefs may be more or less consistent with one another. In a less primitive society, divided into classes, this may be true of people who belong to the same class even though the beliefs of different classes differ widely. The persons who hold similar beliefs may not be aware that they are consistent, for consistency may mean little or nothing to them, and yet their beliefs may in fact be consistent. In an advanced society, the individual, his mind open to many influences, may never succeed in getting his ideas into good order, and there may be considerable differences between the ideas of persons who belong to the same class. I suggest that one of the important ways in which an advanced society divided into classes differs from a less advanced society, similarly divided, is that, while differences of ideological beliefs *between* classes or other social groups are smaller, differences *inside* them are greater. Group 'ideologies' are less coherent and so too are the beliefs of the individual.

Class ideologies have also become less conservative, because in advanced societies everyone takes the fact of social change for granted. The powerful and the wealthy do so no less than others. No doubt, they want to retain their advantages, their wealth and their power, but they cannot hope to do so by preventing change. On the contrary, the demands they make on the government as they pursue their interests are as powerful a cause of social change as the demands made by the poor. The belief (in my opinion, a mistaken one) that the wealthy and powerful, the dominant social groups, are more than the others opposed to change, is due to the fact that changes made in their interest are often considered small or superficial for no other reason than that they leave these groups as powerful as they were. For example, no matter how great the changes made in the American or British economy in response to the demands of the wealthy, everyone, not excluding the wealthy, still calls that economy 'capitalist'. In the past, of course, the wealthy and powerful were, if not the sole, then much the most important initiators of change. Now that the poorer classes are better organized and more demanding than they used to be, the wealthy sometimes look upon themselves as defenders of the established order against them. The changes they favour seem to them (and even to others) more in keeping with 'tradition' than the changes they oppose. But this may be a mistake. Who defines tradition? Who decides what is in keeping with it and what is not? Usually, the dominant groups, who are much better placed than the others to innovate without seeming to do so. I suggest that today in the rich democracies of the West, no social class is much more conservative (more resistant to social change) than another. This, of course, does not imply that as much can be said of social groups that are not classes; some of them may be much more radical or revolutionary than others. Nor does it imply that ideological differences are unimportant, or less important than they used to be.

I said earlier that where classes are highly exclusive (for example, where they are estates or castes) their ideologies tend to be less social and political and more religious than where they are not. Yet I doubt whether religion has ever, to any but a small extent, been class ideology; that is to say, whether important religious beliefs have ever been widely held by a class because they served to maintain or produce conditions and practices favourable to its interests or expressing attitudes and sentiments typical of its members. Even in primitive societies religious beliefs do more than help maintain the social order; they also meet moral and psychological needs of the individual. These needs, to be sure, are peculiar to men, the only rational beings known to us, whose capacity to reason is developed in them by social intercourse. They are therefore needs peculiar to social beings. But from this it does not follow that the beliefs that meet these needs come to be widely held primarily because they help to maintain the social order. No doubt, the beliefs vary considerably from society to society, and even (though less so) from class to class, but they vary also from person to person, regardless of class. Though religious beliefs do often justify the established order, they mostly do so irrespective of the kind of order it is. They seldom justify what is distinctive about it; they often do little more than argue that its long endurance is evidence that God approves of it. Where a religion accepted by all classes teaches obedience to established authority in a society dominated by one class, are we to call it the ideology of the dominant class? Can beliefs shared by all classes constitute a class ideology?

Some people, and not only Marxists, speak as if they could. If the beliefs encourage behaviour that helps to maintain the social order, and that order enables one class to exploit the others, then the beliefs are, or form part of, the ideology of the exploiting class. But the beliefs may have come to be generally accepted before that social order, enabling one class to exploit the others, arose. Besides, the beliefs may be more widely held among the exploited than among their exploiters. Are we still to say that they are the class ideology of the exploiters? If we do say it, we have the paradox of a class ideology less widely held by the class whose ideology it is than by other classes.

Given their aims and the conditions of their achieving them, it may be in the interest of a group to hold some beliefs rather than others. If they hold them regardless of whether or not they are true, they are ideological beliefs. They are both ideological and beliefs of the group. But suppose it is in the interest of a group that other groups should hold certain beliefs and this group is able to ensure that the others do hold them? Are the beliefs a group or class ideology? They are taught because they encourage behaviour that favours the interests of the group. The teachers themselves may not hold the beliefs but must at least pretend to hold them if they are to teach successfully. The beliefs are taught on account of their effects, and neither teachers nor taught examine them critically. They are invoked on appropriate occasions. All this, perhaps, is enough to make them ideological. But is it enough to warrant our calling them the ideology of the group whose interests they favour? I put this question without attempting to answer it. My purpose is not to advise people how they should use the terms 'group ideology' and 'class ideology' but to consider how they are used and some of the problems that arise when their uses are more closely examined.

Though religion is not class ideology, religious beliefs can form part of class ideologies and are sometimes considerably affected by class interests. Religious beliefs that arose before a social order emerged are sometimes adapted to it. For example, they are modified in ways that serve to justify certain practices of the dominant class or to reconcile the poorer classes to their lot. The religious beliefs of different classes can differ considerably even in a society where there is only one 'church' teaching an ortho-dox body of doctrines. Some of the doctrines come to mean much more to some classes than to others, and there are also religious beliefs that are widely held even though they are not orthodox. For unorthodox beliefs often pass unnoticed by the guardians of orthodoxy so long as they are not used to challenge orthodoxy. Uniformity of beliefs is scarcely ever aimed at, let alone achieved. It may be that small, primitive and homogeneous societies come close to having it without aiming to do so. But in primitive soci-eties there are no churches, no guardians of religious orthodoxy. Nor are there guardians of political orthodoxy. Uniformity of belief is valued and sought after only in societies that have moved a long way from it, and the most they ever achieve is uniformity of outward respect for orthodoxy or for the official ideology.

In the West in recent centuries ideological beliefs have come to be predominantly about society and government. Or, per-haps I should say, that men, while they have continued to look to religion to meet their more personal 'moral' needs, have turned increasingly to other than religious beliefs to uphold or condemn established practices or to justify aspirations typical of social classes or other groups. They have also taken their be-liefs, more than their ancestors did, from books and pamphlets, from deliberately produced social and political theories. These

theories have been mostly of two kinds.* Some have started with
the individual, attributing particular wants and skills to him
and arguing that, given that he has them, there are claims
which he can reasonably make on his fellow men, provided that
he is willing to meet similar claims made on him. They have
then gone on to explain (and to justify) the established order on
the ground that it satisfies these wants and claims, or else have
argued that some different order would satisfy them better, and
have advocated either moderate change or change so rapid and
sweeping as to be 'revolutionary'.

Other theories, instead of attributing particular skills and
wants to the individual and arguing for fundamental rights, have
conceived of mankind as involved in a course of change in
which men's wants, skills and claims alter from stage to stage of
the course. Often, though not always, they present the course as
a progress; men's capacities are the more 'fully developed' the
further they are on this course, and their wants and claims
change as their capacities develop. These theories do not all take
it for granted that progress is inevitable, that nothing can inter-
rupt it or throw men back to an earlier stage, but many of them
do imply that mankind tend always to move forward. This
movement, though often impeded, always reasserts itself.

Theories of both these types can serve as class ideologies or
can contribute to them. But it is only theories of the second type
that take account of ideologies and of classes, seeking to explain
how they arise and their functions in society.

It seldom happens that some one theory is accepted wholly,
or even in large part, by a class or by its leaders. What ordinarily
happens is that several broadly similar theories have a considerable influence on the 'leaders' of the class, men whose opinions
are respected inside it or who run organizations recruited from

*Theories can be classified in many different ways. The broad division
into two classes that I make here is not more important than others but is
relevant to my purpose. I do not claim that all social and political theories
fall into one or other of these two classes.

it. Ideas taken from these theories are more or less widely accepted by the leaders, and some of the ideas percolate through to the class generally. It is these ideas current among the leaders or more generally among the class, rather than the set theories from which they are taken, that constitute 'the ideology of the class'. The stock of ideas in use by the leaders, who are only a minority of the class, is ordinarily much richer than the stock used by the class generally; and yet, it is properly included in the ideology of the class—if the leaders really do lead the class, if they are trusted by the class generally, if they are genuinely its spokesmen. The ideology of a class, as I said earlier, is not a coherent system of well-defined beliefs, but it is a set of beliefs that can be described and distinguished from the ideologies of other classes.

Even in the most literate and sophisticated of communities not all the beliefs about society and government that gain wide currency in a class or among its leaders come originally from books. This is no less true of the ideologies of wealthier and better educated classes than of the others. Indeed, it quite often happens that the leaders of the poorer and less educated classes get more of their ideas than do other leaders from books written by social and political theorists. This need not mean that they are less trusted by their followers, though it may mean that their policies and arguments are less understood.

Obviously, in highly literate and economically advanced societies the influence of books on all ideological beliefs, and therefore also on class ideologies, is great. There are many books, there are many ideas in circulation about all aspects of social life and social change. There are many more people than there are in illiterate and backward societies with some understanding of how society functions and how it changes. So the beliefs that constitute the ideology of a class (or of any other considerable social group) are relatively sophisticated. They are so largely because those who hold them must take some notice of beliefs that are not ideological, beliefs about matters social and political that are accepted in all classes and social groups by persons who can appreciate the arguments and the evidence that support them. Again, in societies where class ideologies are sophisticated, people recognize that there are such ideologies. There are widely held beliefs about them and about their origins and effects, and many of these beliefs are not confined to any class. They are neutral beliefs. Even the theorists who deny that there are such beliefs about social phenomena resort to them when they seek to explain what ideology is and how the ideology of one class differs from that of another.

I have spoken several times of people accepting beliefs largely because they further their interests. This is a convenient but also misleading way of speaking. It is misleading if it suggests that interests determine beliefs rather than the other way about, for they affect one another. People who have similar interests are apt also to have similar beliefs about matters relating to these interests, and these interests and beliefs predispose them to accept some new beliefs rather than others about these matters. But their interests are also affected by beliefs about extraneous matters. This is only another way of saying that the interests of classes and groups are affected, sometimes profoundly, by beliefs that form no part of their class or group ideologies. Again, beliefs typical of a class need not support class interests; they may come to be typical of the class because they express feelings or attitudes widely shared inside it but not outside it. These beliefs, too, form part of the ideology of the class, and often an important part. It is worth noticing that the feelings and attitudes expressed by these beliefs may harm the interests of the persons who hold them. A class ideology can be a heavy burden on the class that bears it.

Class-consciousness

A class (and as much is true of any social group) can have an ideology without being class-conscious. Beliefs may be widely held within it because they favour interests or express feelings shared by its members generally, but this the members may not know. Indeed, they may not even be aware that they belong to that class.

Marx, in an often-quoted passage of the *Eighteenth Brumaire*, explained why, in his opinion, the peasants in France lacked class-consciousness. They thought and spoke of themselves as peasants, and this Marx knew. He also knew, presumably, that they had wants, ambitions and sentiments typical of their class. At least, he did not deny it. Nor did he deny that they were aware that these wants and sentiments, or some of them, were peculiar to peasants. In a quite ordinary and allowable sense of the word, the French peasants were class-conscious. They also had a class ideology. There were beliefs widely held among them but rare outside their class which justified them in the pursuit of their ambitions, or expressed fears, resentments and other feelings confined largely to them. Marx was not concerned to deny that they had such beliefs.

Why, then, did he say that they were not class-conscious? Because they were not organized to promote their class interests. Because they did not act together as a class. They had no common purposes, social or political; they had only wants and feelings typical of their class. Speaking of the urban workers, the proletariat, Marx said that they would not be aware of their 'true', their 'objective', class interests until they were class-conscious. His denial of class-consciousness to the peasants therefore implies that they were not aware of the 'objective' interests of their class. Marx perhaps went further than this. He seems to have doubted whether the peasants ever could be class-conscious; and he may have believed that the bourgeois and the proletarians were the only classes capable of achieving class-consciousness. Lukacs certainly believed this, and more besides. For he argued, in *History and Class Consciousness*, more explicitly than Marx ever did, that the proletariat would achieve eventually a fuller consciousness than was possible even to the bourgeoisie. I refer to these beliefs of Marx and of Lukacs only because they raise important and relevant issues.

Someone who said of a class that it did not know its objective interests might mean only that it had mistaken beliefs (or no beliefs at all) about the conditions most favourable to achieving aims typical of the class. But this, it would seem, is not what Marx meant. For he believed that the urban workers, in the process of becoming class-conscious, cease to have the aims they had before the process began. They are educated and changed in the course of their struggle against their exploiters. They organize themselves in the first place to achieve the more obvious and immediate of their common interests. But the experience they gain in pursuit of these interests enlarges their understanding of society and of the situation of their class inside it. They see that situation and their fight against their exploiters in historical perspective. They see that they are an exploited class and will continue to be so while the capitalist economy and the social order that incorporates it endure. They therefore come eventually to aim at revolution, at putting an end to the established order. But the ambitions typical of their class before they become a militant class were bound up with that order. In rejecting that order they reject also these ambitions. Though Marx does not say this in so many words, it is, I think, clearly implied by his account of the proletariat as a revolutionary class. In the process of becoming class-conscious and revolutionary, the workers reject the values of the society they want to destroy. From this it follows that they reject those of their aims that have no meaning apart from these values, or at least that their motive for seeking to destroy the established order is not the absurd hope of achieving these aims.

Marx's idea of the proletarian revolution, unless I have misunderstood it, is not utilitarian. Nor does he imagine the workers, in the course of their struggles, acquiring new personal ambitions, new aspirations for themselves and their families, not to be achieved while the old order endures. The workers, as they become class-conscious and revolutionary and aware of the objective interests of their class, do not come to any such conclusion as this: We now have aims for ourselves different from those of our fathers, and we have learned by bitter experience that we cannot achieve them unless this capitalist economy gives way to one that is socialist. We must therefore strive by all means in our power, including if need be the use of force, to replace capitalism by socialism.

Rather, they conclude that they must destroy the capitalist system, which has become intolerable to them, and set up something better in its place. But just what this something better will be, just how it will be organized, just how men will live inside it, what they will want for themselves, they do not know beforehand. They will discover it only after the revolution, as they strive to solve the problems which then face them. The objective class interests of the revolutionary proletariat do not consist of definite personal aims typical of members of the class, nor of definite social conditions which they correctly believe to favour the achievement of such aims. The revolutionary workers achieve class-consciousness, and are aware of the true interests of their class, when they understand what sort of system capitalism is, how it arises, what it does to people; when they are resolved to put an end to it and are organized to achieve this aim and know how to achieve it. They are class-conscious when they are able and willing to destroy the system and to give mankind a chance to put in its place a social order in which no one is exploited or alienated. But just what this order will be and how men who are no longer exploited and alienated will live, they do not know. It is knowledge to be won after the revolution; and yet the workers must become class-conscious and aware of the objective interests of their class in order to make the revolution.

Marx's ideas about class-consciousness, and especially proletarian consciousness, were taken up and developed by Georg Lukacs. He spoke of the bourgeois and the proletarians as the pre-eminently class-conscious classes, and yet insisted, for all that, that the bourgeois are necessarily caught up in illusion. Their typical aims are definite enough. They want to maintain and, if possible, to increase their profits. They look upon the capitalist economy and the bourgeois state as the conditions of their doing so, and in this they are not mistaken. Nevertheless, Lukacs agrees with Marx that the class-consciousness of the bourgeois is a form of false consciousness. For, though they rightly believe that the maintenance of the established system is in their interest as a class, they also misconceive the system. They cannot understand the 'contradictions' inherent in it, and therefore cannot take effective action to resolve them. For if they understood them and how to resolve them, they would understand that they cannot be resolved except by abolishing the system. But their survival as a class and their pursuit of the personal ambitions typical of them depend on the continuance of the system. Thus, their illusions about the system, their failure to recognize its transience, are necessary illusions; they cannot lose them without losing the will to survive as a class.

Now, according to Lukacs, though it is only the workers who are exploited, the bourgeois also are 'alienated'. They too look upon social relations, which are only ways in which men behave, as if they were things. Instead of controlling them, they look upon them as external forces, largely unpredictable, to which they must resign themselves. So we, who are not Marxists, are tempted to ask: How is it that they too do not come to recognize their predicament and to wish to put an end to it by putting an end to the system in which it is rooted? If man, who is *essentially* a progressive being, is 'alienated' in social and cultural conditions which are only his own ways of behaving and thinking, and if experience teaches him to overcome this alienation and these conditions, why should it not teach the bourgeois as much as the proletarian? Because, so Lukacs implies, it is not his interest as a bourgeois to learn. But this means only that, if he does learn, he then wants to put an end to the system on which the survival

5

of his class depends. The same is true, presumably, of the prole-tarian. If we can say of the one class that it is in its class interest to abolish the system on which the identity of the class depends, why cannot we say it of the other? This, perhaps, is an odd way of using the expression 'class-interest', but no odder in the one case than the other. If someone were to say to us, 'It is Jane's interest *as a wife* to get a divorce', we might—unless she had two husbands—find the expression odd but we should let it pass. But if he were to say, 'Though it is the interest of husbands as husbands to get divorced, it is not the interest of wives as wives', we should feel entitled to an explanation. And if we got the answer, 'Well, look, if wives get divorced, they cease to be wives', we should be disappointed.

Lukacs admits that a bourgeois may come to understand the system and to desire its suppression. If he does, he opts out of his class. Why? Is it because he does what most bourgeois will not do? Lukacs does not explain why this should be so. It does not follow that it must be so merely because the bourgeois are exploiters, and the workers are exploited. Not if both classes are alienated and man is a *progressive* being, in the sense understood by Lukacs and Marx.

Let us get away, for a moment, from the bourgeois and the proletarians, for there are deep-rooted and dark beliefs about them that get in the way of clear thinking. Let us imagine two societies, one with bankers and butchers in it, the other with neither. In the first society bankers are rich and powerful, while butchers are not. In the second society, which is egalitarian and vegetarian, the people generally lead fuller and more varied lives and enjoy life more than anyone does in the first. In the first society bankers have ambitions typical of their profession, which they can achieve without ceasing to be bankers, and the same is true of butchers. There are social conditions, different for each profession but not necessarily incompatible, that favour bankers or butchers in the pursuit of their ambitions. That is to say, bankers and butchers have distinct group interests within the established order. They also have beliefs in line with their interests or which express attitudes typical of their group; they have group ideologies.

Let us suppose that a deeper understanding of the course of social change and of what is involved in man's being essentially progressive moves anyone who acquires it to reject the first society and to want to put the second in its place, and that this understanding comes, not of book-knowledge and solitary meditation, but of working together with other men to achieve common interests. Why should butchers be more likely than bankers to acquire this understanding? Is it because they soon discover that they can do very little, within the existing social order, to ensure that butchers are as wealthy and powerful as bankers? But bankers are better educated than butchers are, and are better placed to study the course of social change. Why should their being richer and more powerful than butchers stand in the way of their discovering that there is something within the reach of all men that is better worth having even than what bankers now have?

To say that a banker who discovers this ceases to be typically a banker is to imply that most bankers will not discover it. Whoever says this must explain why it is so. If he argues that bankers are well off as they are and therefore have no incentive to discover it, he assumes that they are so attached to the standards of their group that experience and reflection will not detach them. Why should not the same be true of butchers? Why should they not be equally attached to the standards of their group? Why should they expect to be anything but butchers? Or, if there are standards common to bankers and butchers making the lot of a banker better than that of a butcher in the eyes of both groups, why should not butchers aspire to be bankers? And if they find that they cannot become bankers, no matter how hard they try, and therefore decide to destroy the established order so as to put all men on a level, why should it be supposed that this decision has anything to do with a deeper understanding of the course of social change and of man as a progressive being?

On the other hand, if there really is this deeper understanding and man really is a progressive being, and if bankers are also alienated, even though they are richer, better educated and more powerful than butchers, why should they be so attached to the standards of their group or of the community that experience and reflection cannot detach them? If the 'objective interests' of butchers are the aims they acquire when they have gained this deeper understanding, why should not bankers also have 'objective interests'? They will, of course, be the same as the 'objective interests' of the butchers; which means that they will not be group interests. They will not be the interests of bankers as bankers or of butchers as butchers, but human interests to be realized in a society where there are neither bankers nor butchers.

Lukacs, like Marx before him, takes it for granted that learning to act together to defend their immediate interests has a quite different effect on the workers from what it has on the bourgeois because they are the exploited class, and are also the more alienated. The conclusion seems to him to follow so obviously that there is no need for further argument. He assumes that, however much the workers' conditions improve under capitalism, they will never improve so much that the workers acquire interests and an ideology in keeping with the established order. He assumes, further, that society will not change in such a way that it ceases to be capitalist without becoming socialist, and he raises no awkward questions about the identity of classes. John Smith, on his sixtieth birthday, is very unlike what he was sixty days after his birth; he is not recognizably the same person and yet he is the same person. But when does a class cease to be? We may define it in terms of the social relations in which its members stand, or in terms of their typical aims, or in terms of their beliefs; but these three things all change continually. When we are in the mood for definition, we select, no doubt, social relations or aims or beliefs that change slowly; but even they change in the end so much that the persons who have them constitute a new class.

If we take a class (or other social group) and define it broadly in terms of some of the social relations in which its members stand, we can then perhaps discover aims typical of the class and define the conditions most favourable to their achievement, consistent with the class retaining its identity. These conditions we can call the 'objective interests' of the class, and we can say that the class is 'class-conscious' when its members are effectively organized to further their interests and have beliefs (an ideology) which contribute to their furtherance. But if we define its objective interests and its class-consciousness as the aims and beliefs which its members would have if they understood the true significance of the course of history, we may be forced to conclude either that the objective interests and consciousness of all classes are the same or that no class ever achieves a full consciousness. If, like Lukacs, we make bold to claim for one class that it alone is destined to achieve it, we must do something better to support our claim than say repeatedly that it is the most exploited and alienated class.

If we abandon as logically absurd the idea of proletarian class-consciousness, as Lukacs develops it from suggestions made by Marx, we are not thereby precluded from saying of some classes that they are nearer to being class-conscious than others. We can say that they know their interests better. We can say that as a result of acting together to further their interests they become more sharply aware of how they differ from other classes. No doubt, by acting together they change their interests. Nevertheless, it still makes sense to say that they know their new interests better than they knew their old ones, and that they are more class-conscious because they have a sharper, fuller and more adequate image of their class. In this respect classes and other social groups are like individuals; as they acquire a fuller and more precise image of themselves, they are changed, which does not prevent the new image being nearer the new truth than the old image to the old truth.

The smaller a social group, the more likely that a high proportion of its members will be group-conscious. Classes are ordinarily very large groups. That is why a class is reckoned to be class-conscious if it has leaders whose right to speak for it is recognized by the class and the leaders are class-conscious. We cannot stop to enquire what constitutes good evidence that the claim of some persons to speak for others is recognized by the others. This is a difficult question, to be discussed at considerable length if it is to be worth discussing at all. Though people differ in their assessments of the claims of particular leaders or groups of leaders to speak for their followers, they agree that such claims are sometimes true and sometimes false. For some purposes—as, for example, for certain legal purposes under international law—leaders who contrive, no matter how, to get their followers to do what they require of them are accounted their spokesmen. But leaders of a class or of a nation who do no more than this are not their spokesmen, in any but a legal sense. Everyone, not excluding even Hitler or Stalin, is agreed about this; for no leader, however harsh, rests his claim to speak for his people on his mere ability to get them to do what he wants by whatever means. Whatever Stalin thought of Stalin, he admitted that leaders who claim to speak for a class sometimes claim what is false. The admission is implicit in his attacks on working-class leaders in the West as lackeys of the bourgeoisie.

If the claim of leaders to speak for a class is false, then the class is not to be reckoned highly class-conscious merely because the leaders know what they are aiming to do, and have an elaborate theory to justify their aims, and have organized the class effectively to ensure that these aims are achieved.

6/The Political Uses of Ideology

Ideology, to many people, means above all the doctrines that political parties and other organizations are committed to, or which they use in their endeavours to get power and influence. In this sense, it is deliberately formulated and exploited; it is what most people have in mind when they speak of indoctrination. But they do not think of it as altogether invented by the parties and other organized groups that make use of it; they think of it as connected with, as feeding upon, ideology in a broader and looser sense. Parties and other groups appeal to some classes or sections more than to others, and their doctrines, if they are to be attractive, must be in keeping with the beliefs, attitudes and aspirations of those classes or sections. Thus ideology, in the narrower 'political' sense, feeds upon ideology in the broader and looser sense. Indeed it not only feeds upon it but also helps to transform it. This interaction between 'political' and 'popular' ideology, though often noticed, has never been studied.

Marxists, for example, think of the doctrines of 'bourgeois' parties as somehow arising out of beliefs and attitudes shared by a whole class, and yet do not deny that the doctrines react upon the beliefs and attitudes. They admit that the doctrines do more than just serve to hold together the class organizations whose doctrines they are, and admit also that they affect the thinking of the class, how its members see the society they belong to and their place in it. And class ideology, taken as a whole in both its 'political' and 'popular' aspects, somehow 'reflects' the interests of the class. All this the Marxists either assert or imply, but they do it without explaining just how class ideologies 'reflect' class interests, or how the doctrines of organized groups are related to the beliefs and attitudes of classes.

According to Marx, bourgeois ideology is 'false consciousness'; it consists of, or rests on, illusions; but the beliefs of the proletarians are not, or need not be, illusory. It is not with them, as it is with the bourgeois, against their class interests that they should see the world, especially the social world, for what it is. This Marxist dispensation in favour of the proletarians has been rejected by later thinkers, whose ideas about ideology, its social functions and political uses nevertheless owe a great deal to Marx.

Where Marx and his disciples speak of 'ideologies', Pareto speaks of 'derivations' and Sorel of 'myths'. Pareto and Sorel differ from Marx and the Marxists in two important respects: their 'derivations' or 'myths' do not 'reflect' class interests, and no class or group in society is peculiarly exempt from illusion. Their differences from Marx are worth considering in some detail, for they illustrate ways of thinking about ideology that are common today, especially among political writers who are not Marxists.

Myths and spurious aims

Pareto's 'derivations' and Sorel's 'myths' are sets of beliefs or doctrines that serve to justify and, to some extent, to direct the actions of groups. These actions, according to Pareto, spring from 'instincts' that 'correspond' to what he calls 'residues'; and by residues he means what is common to theories, whose contents differ but whose functions are the same, when what they owe to circumstances of time and place is eliminated. According to Sorel, they spring from 'impulses'. We need not pause to consider more particularly what Pareto meant by 'residues' (which, in any case, is not clear), nor how what he called 'instincts' differ from the 'impulses' of Sorel. I shall speak, without more ado, of instincts and impulses, even though Pareto used the word 'instinct' in a broader and looser sense than students of human, or even animal, behaviour now think proper.

Though Pareto believed that these instincts are found among men at all times, he said that they are stronger in some men than in others. The actions proceeding from them, and therefore also the 'derivations' that justify and direct these actions, differ according to circumstances. For how an instinct takes effect in action must depend to a large extent on the situations of the persons whom it impels to act. The same is true, presumably, of Sorel's impulses.

Both Pareto and Sorel took it for granted that the actions proceeding from these instincts or impulses are, for the most part, non-rational (or 'non-logical' as Pareto put it). It is not clear why they did so. Men can, and often do, act on impulse, without taking thought, and so act non-rationally. But their 'instincts' and 'impulses', the non-rational springs of action in them, also give rise to conscious desires and thence to purposes. Provided the purposes are compatible with one another, and the actions are intelligently directed towards achieving them, the actions are rational—even though the persons whose actions they are know nothing of the 'instincts' in which their conscious desires and purposes are rooted. There are signs that at least Pareto sometimes recognized that this is so, though he also sometimes forgot it. I shall revert to this point later in another connection.

Neither Pareto nor Sorel, when he spoke of actions sustained by 'derivations' or 'myths', thought of the people concerned as sharing consistent and realistic purposes and coming together to try to achieve them. He thought of them rather as drawn to one another by the need to give effect to 'instincts' and 'impulses' of which they are unaware. Their actions are, of course, an outlet for these instincts and impulses, but the theories they use to justify what they do merely provide excuses for actions whose hidden springs they do not recognize. Sorel, in his own peculiar way, was a radical; he idealized the revolutionary temper and agreed with Marx that the workers are *par excellence* the revolutionary class. He was therefore much concerned with that class, with its activities and myths. But he more or less abandoned the Marxist idea of the workers pursuing their class interests. The revolution, as he conceived of it, is not made in the interest of any class; it merely gives effect to the revolutionary impulse, the impulse to destroy what is felt to be frustrating and degrading, to move into the future unencumbered by the past. The myth justifies the act that proceeds from the impulse. The myth is accepted, not because it has been critically examined and found to be true, nor because it justifies the pursuit of common interests, but because it justifies what those who accept it are impelled to do.

Pareto had no romantic preference for the proletariat. Socially, he was a conservative, and politically a liberal. Yet he was not a conservative in the manner of Burke; he did not hold that prejudice and tradition are essentially rational because they embody the lessons of experience, often dearly bought, and so make it possible for succeeding generations to benefit from them without having to do the painful learning over again. Prejudices and the theories built upon them serve rather to justify actions that arise from 'instincts'. What these instincts are, we need not enquire, for it is not them but the actions they give rise to in particular social conditions that 'derivations' (or ideologies) justify and to some extent direct.

Pareto believed that human behaviour is often (perhaps more often than not) 'non-logical' or, as most people have it, 'non-rational'. To support this general verdict he pointed to the fact that it arises from instinct. Yet he also admitted that from some instincts there arise rational activities—for example, science from what he called the 'instinct for combinations'. Unfortunately, it seems not to have occurred to him that as much could be said of all instincts without gain or loss to the general thesis that human behaviour is predominantly not rational since any might give rise to both rational and non-rational behaviour. Take 'instinct' broadly enough (and Pareto appears to have taken it about as broadly as it could be taken), and all human behaviour proceeds from it. We are still left with the need to explain how rational behaviour differs from behaviour that is not rational, and how it happens that most behaviour is not rational—if that is what we believe.

Pareto would presumably have agreed that many human actions are automatic or habitual, and that they ought to be; that, for example, it is no bad thing that people ordinarily blow their noses without first deciding to do so. Perhaps he meant that most human actions that are purposeful are not rational, or are not what the persons whose actions they are take them to be; or he perhaps had in mind only some classes of purposeful actions, as, for example, 'collective' actions that more than one person takes part in.

To be sure, collective actions are made up of individual ones; but we can often distinguish the private aims of the persons who take part in a collective action from the common aims they are supposed to share. Indeed, we do not ordinarily treat the actions of several (or many) persons as a collective action unless we attribute to them some common aim, even though sometimes, when challenged, we readily admit that the attribution is or may be fictitious. Ordinarily, these supposedly shared aims are defined by some person or persons who direct the collective actions, or else by leaders of groups or communities whose members take part in a variety of such actions. Shared aims, whether the sharing is genuine or fictitious, are sometimes well defined so that it is easy to see whether or not they are achieved; but quite often they are broad or ill defined or differently understood by those who are supposed to share them: as, for example, such aims as equality of opportunity or liberty of conscience or social justice.

Now, presumably, according to Pareto, these 'common' aims, even the broadest of them, arise (as all aims do), from 'instincts'. They are apt to be the least precise of aims, and the ones most often supported by 'derivations' or ideological doctrines and theories. It is actions directed ostensibly towards them that are the most likely to be aimless, or to have aims that are not publicly admitted, or that are incompatible or unrealizable. These, presumably, are the actions that Pareto had chiefly in mind when he spoke of non-logical behaviour.

Pareto, like other thinkers who have enlarged upon the lack of reason in human affairs, stopped short of trying to distinguish between different kinds of purposeful action presumably rooted in drives below the level of conscious purpose, and enquiring how far they are or are not rational. Not only do actions differ greatly in this respect, but the same actions can be rational or not, depending on the aims we take account of when we assess them. A collective action in which many persons take part, may, taken as a whole, be aimless, for its acknowledged or official aims may be so vague as not really to be aims at all. Yet everyone taking part in the action may have quite definite private aims and his actions may be intelligently directed towards achieving them. The collective action, as a whole, is aimless and not rational, but the individual actions that make it up are rational. Or, alternatively, there may be several groups among the participants who all have definite aims and who co-operate intelligently in pursuit of them. The individuals or smaller groups who pursue their own aims intelligently may or may not be sceptical about the larger aims, the spurious aims, which they 'share' with others. And, of course, the larger aims need not be spurious.

Pareto did not say that they must be; he merely assumed that, more often than not, they are. He failed, I think, to take sufficient account of the difference between two kinds of aims: the general and the particular. Either kind of aim can be private or common. John can aim at being a just man, and this aim of his is private and general. He may have clear and realistic ideas about what is involved in being a just man or he may not. But John can also aim, along with his neighbours, at improving the quality of justice in the local court. He and his neighbours then

have a common and a general aim, which again may or may not
be definite and realistic. If they aimed at getting some particular
person elected to an office, or at getting a new school built in the
neighbourhood, their common aim would be particular. A
general aim, private or common, is directed towards keeping up
or attaining some standard or principle in some sphere of
action.

General aims are ordinarily less precise than are particular
ones. Whether they are less precise when they are common than
when they are private, I do not know. But there are good reasons
for holding, not only that common general aims are often vague,
but that they ought to be. Often, if they were more precise, it
would be difficult for a large number of people to agree about
them; they would leave no room for manoeuvre and for com-
promise. If they set no limits to what can be done, they are
empty; if they set limits that are too narrow, they are more
frustrating than useful. The pursuit of them is not to be accounted non-rational merely because it is unlike the pursuit of
particular aims. Nor are the beliefs and theories that justify them
to be dismissed as serving to make what is not rational look
rational.

Pareto was no democrat. He was perhaps not against democracy, but he thought it unattainable. Government genuinely
responsible to the people is impossible. Everywhere there is a
governing class, or rather a set of 'élites' who among them take
the important decisions that the masses accept. 'Derivations'
serve, among other things, to justify the established order in the
eyes of the élites and the masses. That order (or some part of it)
is presented to the élites and the masses as promoting ends
vaguely conceived. It is presented differently to different élites
and masses. There are also derivations that subvert the established order. There is a circulation of élites, some giving way to
others. Some 'instincts' are more active in some élites, and even
some masses, than in others. Derivations vary not only with the
'instincts' of the groups that accept them; they vary also with

social and cultural conditions. Since derivations serve to maintain or subvert the established order rather than to promote the vague and largely unattainable aims they put forward, people who accept them are under an illusion. They imagine that they are seriously engaged in pursuing these aims when in fact they are not.

I hope that this is not an unfair account of part of Pareto's doctrine. But, fair to Pareto or not, it gives the gist of a position that many people come close to holding. There is a measure of truth to it, though it is also misleading. 'Common' aims supported by an ideology that is more assented to than understood are quite often so vague as to be empty. It is true that supposedly common aims and the ideologies that sustain them do serve to keep men in power or help them to get it by preserving or winning the support of the masses. Men who have power or who aspire to it often exploit 'common' aims and ideologies they do not believe in to serve their ambitions.

But ideology often does more than hold a community or group together by giving its members the illusion that they have common aims and are pursuing them rationally; it also expresses a preference for certain kinds of aims over others. True, most people give only vague answers to such questions as, 'What do you mean by social justice or by equality of opportunity?' or, 'What social and political conditions must we have to achieve this justice or this equality?' Moreover, the few who give precise answers give different ones. Nevertheless, in a particular country at a particular time, a political party that insists more on 'social justice' or 'equality of opportunity' than on, say, 'freedom' will have different policies and take different decisions from one that gives pride of place to 'freedom'. These words, as political leaders and their followers use and understand them, are labels attached to different aims and actions at different times. Those who use the labels are for the most part unable to define them; and even if they could define them and agreed on the same definitions, we could not, merely from these definitions and the situations in which the leaders have to take their decisions, predict just what decisions they would take. Yet the use of some labels rather than others in a particular situation does confine the users to one rather than another range of possible decisions.

In an earlier chapter, I distinguished two senses of the term 'group interests'. The term is used sometimes to refer to personal or private aims typical of the groups, and sometimes to refer to conditions that favour the pursuit of these aims. If the members of the group know what these conditions are, they are well advised to work together to achieve them as far as possible, or to support leaders who endeavour to achieve them. But in the world as it is, these leaders, if they are to be able to achieve anything, must get the support of other groups besides this one. If leaders were omniscient, they would know what conditions most favour the pursuit of the typical aims of all the groups that support them, but in practice neither they nor their followers have this knowledge. Therefore the ideology of the party or movement they lead rarely consists of beliefs and theories that encourage and justify the pursuit of interests common to all the groups. The political actions of leaders are not nicely (nor even roughly) calculated attempts to further interests common to their supporters; not at least if these interests are taken to be the conditions that most favour the typical aims of the groups they lead.

Perhaps this was why Pareto, who was an economist before he was a political theorist, was so ready to believe that political activities are less rational than economic ones. He also noticed, no doubt, that ideology is more conspicuous in politics than in trade and industry. He therefore concluded that in the political sphere ideologies (or derivations) serve, not to define common interests and to guide men in the pursuit of them, but to hold leaders and followers together. But this is only a part of the truth. Political ideology, for all its vagueness, affects people's conceptions of the 'common' interests of the groups they belong to, and also (though less directly) their private aims. Even though there is no aim shared by all the supporters of a party other than its getting power, the party's ideology, the principles and sentiments that its leaders proclaim and the more general arguments used to justify its policies, have a considerable influence both on the demands made on the party by the groups that look to it for favours and on personal ambitions. These demands and these ambitions are often quite definite. There are within the party many and varied activities directed towards clear and realistic aims not shared by the whole party and yet considerably influenced by its ideology. Nor is the pursuit of these aims necessarily the less rational the more incoherent and unrealistic the ideology that influences them. For ideology is only one among several influences on human behaviour, and that behaviour's being rational depends on its being intelligently directed towards achieving clear and realistic aims—which it can be, however poor the intellectual quality of the ideology that partly inspires it.

In a democracy whose least intelligent citizen was as intelligent as Pareto, we should still expect political ideologies to be vague and the supporters of a party to have few aims in common beyond the wish that the party should do well at elections. It would be unreasonable to expect more, especially if the democracy were as large as Italy and its citizens were to enjoy as much freedom as Pareto wanted for himself.

The exploitation of ideology

The pure Machiavellian, who exploits the passions, needs and beliefs of others ruthlessly for his own ends, does not exist. Yet there is something Machiavellian about all successful leaders, even the few saints among them. Exploitation is not always selfish. The leader who aims at what he honestly believes is desirable does not confine himself always to rational persuasion; he sometimes tries to get people to do what he wants by arguments which he does not himself find convincing. The exploiter of beliefs may hold the beliefs he exploits or he may not, though to some extent he usually does. His exploitation of beliefs consists in his using them to get others to do what he wants by uses which he believes are logically unsound, or would believe to be so if he stopped to consider them. He is concerned to persuade but cares little or nothing for the soundness of the arguments he uses. Sometimes, indeed, he wants, not to persuade others, but to corner them, to put them in a position where they dare not disagree openly or refuse to do what he asks, or cannot do so without ruin to themselves. Stalin delighted in treating his opponents in this way; he wanted to humiliate or crush them, and not to win them over.

The exploitation of beliefs occurs in many situations, and the beliefs exploited are often not ideological. Yet ideological beliefs lend themselves more than others do to systematic exploitation on a large scale. What in our time we have learned to call 'ideological warfare' is to a large extent a systematic exploitation of beliefs; and never more, or never more ruthlessly so, than inside an organized group, a party or a church, or a community whose leaders accept an elaborate and carefully formulated body of doctrines. Some of these doctrines may be so obscure that nobody knows what those who accept them are committed to believing and yet the skill and care devoted to their wording may be immense. The doctrines may be unintelligible, and yet a great deal may turn on who wins an argument about how they should be worded, and the argument may call for great ingenuity, self-control and courage.

In Voltaire's day, the enemies of the Roman Church sometimes spoke of it as if it were a cynical conspiracy to take advantage of ignorance and credulity. It taught, so they said, beliefs which many of its priests, especially the exalted in the hierarchy, did not themselves hold, though they professed to do so. These beliefs encouraged hopes and fears that the Church could exploit to enrich itself and maintain its power. This attack on the Church was not confined to unbelievers; it was made also by Christians who accused the priests of abusing their authority by teaching beliefs that were not part of the faith. Attacks of this kind on organized teaching bodies have long been made, and have taken many forms. The attackers have not always doubted the sincerity of the priests and other teachers attacked by them but have accused them of being as much concerned to get power as to propagate beliefs which they held to be true and important.

Implicit in many of these attacks is a distinction between two kinds of activity which, since they are both forms of teaching, have much in common. I shall call one 'instruction' and the other 'indoctrination'. Imparting skills that are useful generally (for example, reading and writing), or in particular occupations or activities, imparting factual information which is useful in similar ways, expounding theories or historical explanations recognized to be provisional (to be accepted only so long as they stand up to criticism, especially by experts), teaching people to observe rules that are generally observed: all this is 'instruction'. 'Indoctrination' is the teaching of beliefs (which the teacher may or may not share) to ensure, not that people carry on competently their social roles and occupations, or activities of their own choosing, or avail themselves of the opportunities society has to offer, or that they behave tolerably well by standards generally accepted in the community or in the circles they move in, but that they think and behave in ways that the teacher thinks desirable or that suit some purpose of his own.

I am aware that I have made what is at best only a rough distinction, but I hope it is sufficient for my purpose. Sometimes it is virtually impossible to decide whether a teacher (or persuader or informant) is instructing or indoctrinating. Some people would say that there is unavoidably an element of indoctrination in some forms of instruction, if the two are defined as I have defined them. Does not the teacher who teaches people to observe rules that are generally observed also teach them to behave in ways that he thinks desirable? No doubt, he often does, but not always. To prepare someone to be a tolerable neighbour is one thing; to try to make him the sort of person that you think he ought to be is another. The first activity passes easily into the second, and it is often impossible to tell them apart. Often but by no means always. My purpose, in any case, is only to make a rough distinction, though an important one, between two activities—both of them forms of teaching in the broad sense of that word—of which one aims at preparing people for the roles, occupations and opportunities that fall to their lot or that they choose, and the other at getting them to think or feel or act in ways that the teacher thinks good or favourable to his purposes.

To indoctrinate is not in itself to exploit belief. The indoctrinator may believe that the doctrines he teaches are true and may want others to accept them because they are true, or he may want them to accept rules which he thinks are right. No doubt, he wants them to act on the beliefs and to conform to the rules; he wants to achieve, or to preserve, a state of affairs in which men do act on these beliefs and conform to these rules. He may even, sometimes, use arguments which he does not himself find convincing to get people to accept beliefs and rules which he himself accepts; he may not be an altogether disingenuous persuader. Nevertheless, in so far as these are his aims, in so far as he wants others to accept what he accepts, he is not yet an exploiter of beliefs; he is merely an indoctrinator.

But if he tries to get people to accept beliefs (or to seem to do so) for some purpose which he does not disclose to them, even one that they later come to approve, he is an exploiter of beliefs. He wants to do more than get people to accept what he believes to be true or right, for he has an ulterior motive. It is his having it, and not his lack of faith in what he teaches (for, as we have seen, he may have faith in it) that makes him an exploiter. He is an exploiter, no matter how good his ulterior motive.

The exploitation of belief is no new thing. Nor has it gone unnoticed until quite recent times; there are references to it scattered in the writings of political philosophers and historians. But with the spread of literacy it has become more systematic.

pervasive and ingenious than it used to be, and also bolder and
more ambitious, if not more cynical. The priests whom the
philosophers two centuries ago accused of exploiting religion
had to make do with beliefs that had been around for many
centuries. Their stock-in-trade was inherited from the past; they
could add little to it. Their philosophical accusers spoke of
Christianity not so very differently from the way that Lucretius
had spoken of earlier religions in *De Rerum Natura*. It consisted
(in their eyes) of beliefs surviving from the childhood of the race
which the spread of knowledge and of literacy would dissipate.
They thought of the priests as fighting a losing battle against
reason. Even the writers who favoured Christianity, who thought
of it as a support of morality, spoke of it as a store of wisdom to
be preserved but not added to. Both the enemies and the friends
of Christianity thought of its doctrines as passing virtually unchanged from generation to generation. To the enemies it was
an old, old burden to be lifted at last from the shoulders of men,
and to the friends a treasure for perennial use. Machiavelli,
whose conception of religion was in some ways very like our
conception of ideology, who praised the founders of some of the
older religions for a wisdom which he took to be essentially
political, spoke of this 'gift' of theirs to the people as something
to be preserved piously and kept pure like their fundamental
laws.

Machiavelli believed that any ruler worth his salt would not
scruple to publish lies and to suppress the truth if to do so helped
him to achieve his aims. The dissemination of opinions, false and
true, has long been accepted as one of the essential arts of government. The ruler cannot help but tell lies, but he ought to be, in
his own and his country's interest, a prudent and skilful liar. He
should preserve as far as he can his reputation for veracity. He
must get people to believe what it suits him that they should by
his adroit handling of the truth, and must resort to lies only
when he cannot otherwise attain some object really worth
attaining.

This politic lying and skilful handling of the truth, though it exploits beliefs, need not be an exploitation of ideology. For the beliefs it exploits may not be ideological; they may not form sets of beliefs that people resort to in certain kinds of situation, nor serve to encourage or discourage types of behaviour, nor express typical sentiments and attitudes. To publish official information, true or false, or to put about rumours, is of course deliberately to create beliefs; but unless the beliefs are ideological, their dissemination, no matter what the purpose behind it, is not an exploitation of ideology.*

Machiavelli, the first of the great political writers to take into account and to advocate the exploitation of beliefs, had in mind only calculated uses and abuses of information. He had nothing to say about the political uses of ideology. He had, of course, a great deal to say about the usefulness of religious beliefs and practices, but he thought of them rather as serving to maintain social ties and as supporting morals than as things to be exploited in the getting of power and the promoting of policy. The founder of a religion is even more to be admired, Machiavelli tells us, than the founder of a state, if the religion strengthens ties and motives that preserve the community; but the establishment of religion, as he conceives of it, is more like education than it is like the use of ideology as an instrument of policy.

It was above all the French Revolution that brought home to political theorists that ideology (though they had not yet learned to call it by that name) could be used deliberately to achieve power or other political ends. It was brought home, for example, to Edmund Burke and to Benjamin Constant. Burke, in his attack on the French revolutionaries, made an elaborate defence of what he called 'prejudice'. Prejudices, according to his idea

*Sometimes beliefs not in themselves ideological are more readily accepted by people who have a certain ideology than by others; for example, by Catholics or by Communists more readily than by Protestants or by liberals. The disseminator of such beliefs can perhaps be said to exploit an ideology if part of his motive for disseminating them is the conviction that they will go down well with persons having that ideology.

of them, are widely accepted and long-established beliefs that hold society together; most people accept them unquestioningly, and the maintenance of social order requires that they should do so. These beliefs can be justified, for they are fruits of experience; they embrace the practical wisdom of the community, and are passed on from generation to generation, so that each succeeding generation need not undergo a painful learning of them directly from experience but can take them on trust. These beliefs, though they form a coherent system, are not the products of deliberate theorizing, and the proper business of the theorist is to explain and justify them and not to seek presumptuously to replace them with something better. But the French revolutionaries were using theories deliberately to undermine these salutary beliefs to help them achieve their ambition to transform France. In other words, they were exploiting ideology. Constant, though less hostile to the revolutionaries than Burke (perhaps because he knew France better), accused them of using the attractive but unrealistic doctrines of Rousseau to impose themselves on their country.

The prejudices that Burke defended are, of course, ideological beliefs in the wide sense of the term; they serve to encourage and discourage types of behaviour and they express typical sentiments and attitudes. But they are not, as he conceived of them, deliberately produced with those ends in view; they do not constitute theories, and the use of them is not an exploitation of ideology. But the French revolutionaries were deliberately using their theories and doctrines so as to get and keep power and achieve their other purposes; they were consciously using them for political ends. This sort of political exploitation of ideology, though by no means confined to the last two centuries, has been during this period much more sustained and massive, and therefore much more widely noticed. Burke and Constant, if they had looked hard enough, could have found many earlier examples of what they deplored in revolutionary France but could hardly have found it on so large a scale and so consciously done.

What they deplored was soon taken as a matter of course, as an activity inevitable in large and advanced societies, and which could do either harm or good. To denounce it indiscriminately was absurd; the point was rather to understand it, and to prevent or oppose it when it was harmful. As social and political theorists looked more closely at the political uses of ideology, their beliefs about them gained in sophistication and realism.

Marx, following the example of earlier socialists, spoke of the doctrines of the French revolutionaries as serving the interests of a class, the bourgeoisie. He called them a class ideology. In fact, they were both more and less than this. Their appeal was not confined to the many different social categories to whom the word 'bourgeois' was applied in France, and they were often used by small groups of ambitious men to support policies that frightened the bourgeois and would have hurt their interests if carried out. They were even used by socialists to justify putting an end to what they called bourgeois society. Therefore, to call these doctrines 'bourgeois ideology' is seriously misleading, even though they did appeal to the bourgeois and were at times used successfully to promote their interests. And yet 'bourgeois ideology' deserves its name a good deal better than what Marxists call 'proletarian ideology' or (to give it the name they sometimes prefer to use) 'proletarian consciousness'. For there is little evidence anywhere that the workers, taken generally, have cared much for the doctrines and sentiments that Marxists have in mind when they speak of proletarian consciousness. If they have appeared to do so anywhere, it has been in countries where the doctrines are propagated by authority and to challenge them is dangerous.

The most powerful ideology of our time, the Communist ideology, which owes as much to Lenin as to Marx, is conspicuously not a class ideology. It comes closer to being an ideology of the *déclassés* who for one reason or another have come to hate the established order, or an ideology of a ruling party imposing its decisions on all social groups. In Russia it began by being the first and later became the second; in the West it is still predominantly the first, even in France and Italy where millions of workers and peasants vote for the Communist Party. These workers and peasants are not, of course, *déclassés* but their leaders often are; and it is they, and not their followers, who take the ideology seriously. It is doubtful whether many Communist voters in the West 'share' the ideology of their leaders even to the extent that many practising Christians 'share' the faith of their priests; it is doubtful whether they even assent to doctrines which for the most part they do not understand. In western countries the vote for the Communist Party is largely a protest vote, and is known to be such by both leaders and voters.

Outside the West, the Communists have gained power in countries where the vast majority of the people know almost nothing of their ideology. To get power they had of course to exploit popular beliefs but these beliefs formed no part of their own creed. Except in the West, where they have not gained power, they have propagated their doctrines extensively only after gaining power. No doubt, they believe, many of them, in these doctrines and want to create a society in which they are applied. But they also propagate them because they believe that they cannot long retain power unless the doctrines are widely accepted. They believe, too, that they must be a united party if they are to gain power and keep it, and that to be a united party they must be united in the creed.

Today, the doctrines of the Communist Party are much more the ideology of an élite than of a class. This is due, above all, to Lenin. Though he looked upon Marxism as the theory of the organized and class-conscious proletariat (an idea of it in keeping with Marx's own conception of the role of theory in the working-class movement), he also looked upon it as the creed of a militant and highly disciplined party. This second idea of it is not taken from Marx. No doubt, Marx believed that the workers must be organized and united against their 'class enemies', and believed also that theories like his own would help them to understand the situation and the interests of their class. But he never imagined the class led by a tightly organized party wedded to a body of doctrine which the party alone could interpret and revise. He never conceived of a party controlling all other 'working-class' groups, and eventually all organized groups of any size in the community it dominated. That ideology might be used to hold a great party tightly together, to justify its elimination of all rivals, and to impose its will on the people generally—this idea of it is not Marxist but Leninist. It did not come to Lenin suddenly; it came to him gradually as he took his chances and argued that he was right to do so.

This idea of Lenin's which does not come from Marx does not come from Pareto either. Yet it is closer, in some ways, to Pareto's ideas about 'élites' and 'derivations' than to anything to be found in the writings of Marx. Pareto used the term 'élite' in a broad sense to refer to any group or category of persons who excel in any way. In this sense, Hitler and his lieutenants were just as much an 'élite' as are the Fellows of the Royal Society. Men and women brought together by a dislike of the established order, by a desire to destroy it and to get power in doing so, and who succeed in their purposes, are an élite. The doctrines they use to justify their efforts and to win support are their doctrines; they are the 'derivations' that enable them to realize their ambitions. Lenin, of course, did not speak of Marxism as Pareto spoke of derivations; he spoke of it and of its significance for the workers as a Marxist might be expected to do. Nevertheless, his actual use of Marxism in controversies with other Marxists, in organizing his party, in making the Bolshevik revolution, in consolidating the party's power after the revolution, fits in more closely with Pareto's account of élites and derivations than with Marx's ideas about classes and class-consciousness.

No exploiter of ideology has been more successful than Lenin. He was a fervent believer in the doctrines he exploited, but a believer with something of the cynic about him. It may be that it takes a believing cynic to be a really able exploiter of beliefs.

The complete cynic feels the power of the beliefs he exploits too little to use them imaginatively as well as boldly, to see what can be done with them. The true believer untouched by cynicism is apt to be too slow to take his chances. The mere stickler for orthodoxy is not really a man of ideas; he is a creature of habit. He cannot make a bold use of ideology in unforeseen circumstances; he is encased in it as in a heavy suit of armour. He is safe inside it while everything is quiet on the intellectual front but feels the burden of it when he has no choice but to bestir himself.

A great advantage of Marxism as ideology is that it presents itself as a theory that develops. Its adepts do not look upon it as a corpus of unchanging doctrines. It has, so they say, implications to be discovered only in the light of experience by those who accept it and try to act upon it. Experience brings them to it in the first place, for it makes better sense of experience than any alternative to it, and yet they continue to learn from experience after they have accepted it. They take in the lessons of experience at a deeper level for having accepted the theory, and experience deepens their understanding of the theory. Thus human experience and the theory that gets to the essence of it stand in a dialectical relation to one another. They do not merely affect one another but each enriches the other. Theory gives meaning to experience and experience gives life to theory. The experience, of course, is a social experience and the theory a shared theory. The evolution of Marxism (or Marxism-Leninism) is not, on their view of it, progress as we find it in the sciences, with investigators, alone or in teams, making their separate and expert contributions to a common and growing store of knowledge. Marxists think of themselves as working together to further the same causes and as sharing the same beliefs. It is the experience they gain as collaborators and co-believers that deepens their understanding of things human and social; it deepens this understanding as the theory which makes it possible is enriched. We have here a marriage of two principles: theory develops in the light of experience, and the truly enlightening experience comes only to those who work together to good purpose because they accept the theory.

This, logically, is an uneasy marriage but it sometimes produces extraordinary results. I have spoken of the Communists, disciples of Lenin who claim also to be disciples of Marx, because in our age they have been the most ruthless exploiters of ideology. But there are other examples.

Ideology has been exploited politically in our time for at least four purposes. It has been used to bring and hold together a disciplined group able to take quick advantage of changing circumstances to achieve power. It has been used to induce people to make great sacrifices for causes which have meant much more to their leaders than to them. It has been used to extend the power of a government or other organized body outside the country or countries in which it already has power. And it has been used inside a party or other organization by people endeavouring to get or to retain control of it. These are not the only uses, not even the only political uses, to which ideology has been put, but they are perhaps the most important.

These uses often inhibit one another. To get power is one thing, and to keep it and use it to achieve some great purpose is another. Those who exploit ideology to get power often do so in ways that make it impossible for them to achieve the purposes for which they originally wanted power. They acquire new purposes which they persuade themselves are still the old ones because they use the old words to describe them. Sometimes the use of an ideology in one part of the world affects it in ways which make it more difficult to use it in other parts. Sometimes, too, the exploitation of an ideology inside a party by groups competing for control of it weakens the appeal of the ideology to people outside the party. We need only look at what the Communists have achieved and failed to achieve in the last fifty years to see how one use of ideology can get in the way of another.

If we wish to understand political behaviour, we do well to

study ideologies and the uses to which they are put. For this study gets us just as close to the realities of politics as the study of group interests and the pursuit of them. Admittedly, people often do not know quite what they believe, and their beliefs are inconsistent with one another; but then, also, they often do not know their interests. Man, the ideological animal, is not less rational than man, the pursuer of interests. The exploitation of ideology for political purposes is difficult and precarious. It is a game that hardly anyone plays successfully for long. Moreover, it can be a game as dangerous as it is difficult. It all depends on how the struggle for power is conducted. It is perhaps a mistake to assume, as Pareto did, that in this game the spectators, the masses, are pre-eminently the victims and the dupes of the players, the élites. Where the game is dangerous to the spectators, it is usually even more dangerous to the players. And, surely, it is the talkers who are the dupes of the talkers; for they not only do all the talking, they do most of the listening as well.

Bibliography

GEERTZ, CLIFFORD, "Ideology as a Cultural System", in *Ideology and Discontent*, edited by David Apter, Free Press, New York 1964.

HEGEL, G. W. F., Preface to *The Phenomenology*, translated by Walter Kaufmann in his *Hegel*, London 1966. It is from Hegel that the concept of ideology as Marx and other German thinkers used it ultimately derives, and *The Phenomenology* is a philosophical account of how men's ideas about themselves and the world develop from stage to stage throughout history. It was first published in 1807.

JOHNSON, HARRY, "Ideology and the Social System", in *International Encyclopaedia of the Social Sciences*, No. 7.

MANNHEIM, KARL, *Ideology and Utopia*, International Library of Psychology, Philosophy and Scientific Method: Harcourt, Brace and World, New York 1955. A book much criticized and still widely read. The first edition of *Ideologie und Utopie* appeared in 1929.

MARX, KARL and ENGELS, FRIEDRICH, *The German Ideology*, Foreign Languages Publishing House, Moscow 1965. The section on Feuerbach is the first Marxist account of the connection between social conditions and ways of thinking. The book was complete by the summer of 1846 and was first published in full in Moscow in 1932.

MERTON, ROBERT K., *Social Theory and Social Structure*, The Free Press, Glencoe, Ill. 1957. Especially Part III, "The Sociology of Knowledge" and Part IV, "Studies in the Sociology of Science".

PARETO, VILFREDO, *Sociological Writings*, selected and introduced by S. E. Finer, translated by Derick Mirfin, Pall Mall Press, London 1966. Especially Part II and the editor's introduction. Pareto's account of the social functions of ideology ('derivations'), though it owes much to Marx, is more elaborate and in important respects different.

POPPER, KARL R., *The Open Society and Its Enemies*, Vol. 2, London 1961 (paperback edition). Especially chapters 23 and 24 and addendum. A criticism of some Marxist and post-Marxist ideas about knowledge.

SHILS, EDWARD, "The Concept and Function of Ideology", in *International Encyclopaedia of the Social Sciences*, No. 7.

SOREL, GEORGES, *Reflections on Violence*, translated by T. E. Hulme and J. Roth, The Free Press, Glencoe, Ill. 1950. Especially II, 1, 2; III, 1, 5. Less systematic than Pareto. *Réflexions sur la violence* first appeared in 1906.

See also:

BIRNBAUM, NORMAN, *The Sociological Study of Ideology, 1940–60; a Trend Report and Bibliography*, Blackwell, Oxford 1962. Prepared for the International Sociological Association with the support of UNESCO.

DE CONDORCET, A., *Sketch for a Historical Picture of the Progress of the Human Mind*, translated by June Barraclough with an introduction by Stuart Hampshire, Library of Ideas, London 1955. A French account, first published in 1795, of the development of knowledge.

LUKACS, GEORG, "Geschichte und Klassenbewusstsein" in Vol. 2 of *Georg Lukacs Werke*, Hermann Luchterhand, Berlin 1968. French translation *Histoire et Conscience de Classe*, Editions de Minuit, Paris 1960. An ambitious development of Marxist ideas about class-consciousness and its social conditions.

WEBER, MAX, *The Methodology of the Social Sciences*, translated and edited by Edward Shils and Henry Finch, The Free Press, Glencoe, Ill. 1949. Discusses "Ethical Neutrality" and "Objectivity" in the social sciences. The essays included in this selection were written between 1903 and 1917.

Index

Alienation, 117*ff.*
Anti-clericalism, 86, 133
Anthropomorphism, 65
Art, 80

Beliefs, 16, 31; beliefs of primitive peoples, 21, 23, 31, 73, 74, 108; belief-systems, 21; descriptive beliefs, 70; explicit and implicit beliefs, 21; persuasive beliefs, 70, 72*ff.*; 'relativity' of, 58*ff.*; socially determined beliefs, 50*ff.*

Burke, Edmund, 126; prejudice, 137; French Revolution, 137

Castes, 102
Class-consciousness, 26, Chapter 5 *passim*
Class ideology, Chapter 5 *passim*
Condillac, Etienne Bonnot de, 15
Constant, Benjamin, and French Revolution, 138
Communism, 45, 79, 106, 139, 140

Descriptive beliefs/theories, 70

Empirical sciences, 61
Engels, Friedrich, 20; proletariat, 26; natural sciences, 62
Enlightenment, the, 85

'False consciousness': *see* under Marx
Feudal societies, 102
French Revolution, 137

Hegel, G. W. F., 20, 32*ff.*; history, 38*ff.*; 'Infinite Mind', 36*ff.*; knowledge, 35*ff.*, 44, 54; language, 36,

44; religion, 88; social order, 41; 'Spirit', 36*ff.*; 'Spirit', objective and subjective, 39*ff.*; *The Phenomenology of Spirit*, 86; *Weltanschauung*, 43*ff.*
Hitler, Adolf, 122, 141
Hobbes, Thomas, 85
Hume, David, and empirical philosophy, 32

'Ideological tale', 76
Ideological warfare, 133
Ideology: class, Chapter 5 *passim*; partial, 18; persuasive, 75; political uses of, Chapter 6 *passim*; prescriptive, 75; sophisticated and unsophisticated, 18; total, 17, 27, 70
Indoctrination, 134
Islam, 85

Kant, Immanuel, 32*ff.*; categories, 33; knowledge, 33*ff.*; religion, 87
Knowledge, 33*ff.*, 44, 54

Language, 36, 44, 61
Lenin, Vladimir Ilyich, 139, 140
Locke, John, 85
Lucretius, *De Rerum Natura*, 136
Lukacs, Georg, and alienation, 117*ff.*; bourgeois consciousness, 27, 114; *History and Class Consciousness*, 27, 114; proletarian consciousness, 27, 114, 116

Machiavelli, Niccolo, 70, 84, 136
Mannheim, Karl, 30, 46*ff.*; *Ideology and Utopia*, 46, 55; knowledge, 53n, 55*ff.*; Marx, 63; 'relativity'